British Miniature Railways

A Photographic Survey

ISBN 1-900622-02-5 (Hardback)

British Library Cataloguing in Publication Data
Knight, Neville R.
British Miniature Railways : a photographic survey
1. Railroads, Miniature - Great Britain - Pictorial works
2. Railroads, Miniature - Great Britain - History
I. Title
385'.0941

Publishing, Typesetting and Design by:
RailRomances, PO Box 85,
Chester. CH4 9ZH

Image Setting and Jacket Design by:
Lazertype, Laurel Bank,
Gresford, Wrexham LL12 8NT

Printed by:
The Amadeus Press Ltd.,
517 Leeds Road,
Huddersfield. HD2 1YJ

British Miniature Railways

by

Neville R. Knight

A photographic survey

PO Box 85, Chester. CH4 9ZH
UK

*Chichester Model Engineers' Golden Jubilee celebrations. One of the highlights at this event was the steaming of their 1908 built 4-4-0 No.1 **Winnie**, a locomotive constructed over a three year period by Mr. Robert Alexander Briggs, AMI Mech. E and his son, Mr. Robert Westrope Briggs. This locomotive is unique in having the cylinders from a steam car. Now a healthy 91 years old, **Winnie** is a great attraction on the 10^1/$_4$ inch gauge railway. Photographed with driver Alan Edwards on 15th August, 1998.*

Foreword

It is now 75 years since I first rode on a miniature railway and every detail of that wonderful day is etched in my memory. This was the 7¼ inch gauge line at the *Beauty Spot*, near Ilkeston (Derbyshire), operated by Louis Shaw and Herbert Ballington and worked by the Atlantic locomotive, built by Shaw in 1918.

On leaving school in 1930, because of the recession at that time, I had to take work very different from that of being involved in miniature railways, which was really what I wanted to do but after six years in the Royal Engineers, on the standard gauge, as fireman and driver, I felt qualified in 1946 to apply for a job as a locomotive driver on the *Romney, Hythe & Dymchurch Railway*.

I stayed with that company for the rest of my working life taking charge of all the locomotives and *Green Goddess* was my regular machine for well over 30 years. The small railway has always been my main interest and just as I always considered it an honour and privilege to work on the R.H.&D.R., I feel the same about being invited to pen these few words.

The author of this labour of love, BRITISH MINIATURE RAILWAYS, is a good friend of mine and we exchange slides and prints in order to keep our photographic records as complete and up to date as possible and I know how much work is involved in maintaining such records. Neville Knight travels many miles every year to record with his camera these small railways in the UK, and I cannot recommend too strongly this splendid "browse" of pictures, taken over the past 30 years or so.

Nor must we forget, as we enjoy this book, the immense pleasure these little railways illustrated have given and will continue to give, to countless folk. We must remember, too, those who made these small railways possible, not forgetting the late Erich Thomsen, who twice, in 1988 and 1992, brought one of his locomotives from the *Redwood Valley Railway*, in California, over 5000 miles to run on 15 inch gauge railways in the UK - events never to be forgotten by miniature railway people on both sides of the Atlantic. We enjoyed equally the epic event of 1993 when Alister Matheson followed Erich's remarkable achievement by travelling half way round the world from Port Arthur in Tasmania to show us his magnificent Garratt Bush Mill 3.

George A. Barlow B.E.M.

Operating Manager (retired)
Romney, Hythe & Dymchurch Railway

May 1999

Appreciation

The idea of producing a fully illustrated book on the subject of *British Miniature Railways* was not as easy as first contemplated. My initial thoughts, jotted down on scraps of paper became a starting point. It was apparent that some input would be necessary beyond what I had already prepared. Various potential readers offered constructive comment and additional information, with general help in many ways.

In particular I mention help from George Barlow with answers to many questions and certain documentation. David Holroyde kindly checked the initial draft pages and his input; so generously offered was most welcome. David Robinson has given tremendous assistance checking the final draft sheets, each one has been examined in minute detail, a special thanks to him as this was a most time consuming task.

Many other people have assisted where special facilities have been requested. My grateful thanks go to Lord Braybrooke who kindly allowed photography on the Audley End Railway; Chris Bishop who obligingly helped, along with Kim Richardson and colleagues, with on site photography at Great Cockcrow, and Colin Cartwright both at Walsall and Betws-y-Coed. Facilities and offers of help in so many ways came from Peter Bowers, Ron Carman, Jack Doyle, John Edgington, Brell Ewart, Neville Fields, Bill Gage, Roger Greatrex, Michelle Greaves, Lady J.Gretton, Laurence Hall, Chris Halsall, Chris W. Heaps, Ian Hickling, Peter James, Quentin Jones, Matthew Kerr, H.G.Merritt, Austin Moss, Brian Nicholson, Jeff Price, Brett Rogers, John Spencer, Jeff Stubbs, Mal Thomas, Simon Townsend, Mike Wadey, Peter Ward, and John Williams. At various locations so many people have helped in positioning locomotives for photography, their assistance too has been most appreciated. My sincere thanks to everyone.

*George Barlow with **Green Goddess** on the Romney Hythe & Dymchurch Railway*

Introduction

My own photographic records of miniature railways commenced about 1962, although I did some early photography on the *Romney, Hythe & Dymchurch Railway* in 1953. A visit to *Belle Vue Railway*, Manchester, 37 years ago directed my interest towards smaller engines. Names like Bassett-Lowke and Barnes were new to me; soon this fascination opened up a new world of miniature railways.

This photographic survey provides a synopsis of past and current events on some of our miniature lines. It does not seek to give a history of the lines, which are from 7¹/₄ to 15 inch gauge and, with one exception, operate at ground level.

The railways featured are open, or have been open to the public, or have open days for visitors. An entry fee may be payable at some locations. None of the photographs were taken at private residences. It should also be understood that some of the railways featured, like other business concerns, do occasionally change their trading names. As far as possible the correct title and terminology have been used.

There are probably about 200 miniature railways in Britain, though not all are steam operated. Some have been established for many years; others are new and developing. Each year there are some closures but happily new lines continue to open. The number and quality of new locomotives is remarkable. I hope my photographs show the diversity and interest to be found in *British Miniature Railways* and encourage readers to see and enjoy these small railways for themselves.

The book has five chapters; each one covers a number of railways of similar gauge; some are based on narrow gauge construction and others very much to scale in design. Each one is different, but provides us with enjoyment just the same.

Over the years I have made many friends amongst miniature railway owners and operators. To them all I owe my thanks for permission to take photographs and for their help and understanding so readily given.

In a few instances the work of other photographers has been used to supplement my own material and this is credited accordingly. The information has been updated to May, 1999.

Neville R. Knight.

Lancashire 1999

The Author and Publisher respectfully indicate that all railways and other locations shown in this publication do not guarantee right of entry to their property now or at any other time, or to specific photographic viewpoints where the public do not have right of access. Permission to enter certain areas which are enclosed or restricted must be obtained by prior application to the railway operator or relevant authorised body.

Contents

Chapter 1
15 inch Gauge

Alton Towers

Belle Vue Railway

Blenheim Park Railway

Bure Valley Railway

Cleethorpes Coast Light Railway

Dreamland Miniature Railway

Dudley Zoo Railway

East Lancashire Miniature Railway

Fairbourne Railway

Gateshead National Garden Festival

Goshen Fields

Haigh Hall Railway

Liverpool International Garden Festival

Kirklees Light Railway

Lakeside Miniature Railway

Lappa Valley Railway

Lightwater Valley Railway

Littlecote Hall Railway

Longleat Railway

Markeaton Park Railway

Paradise Railway

Rail 150 Shildon

Ravenglass & Eskdale Railway

Rhyl Miniature Railway

Romney, Hythe & Dymchurch Railway

Saltburn Miniature Railway

Steamtown Miniature Railway

Sutton Miniature Railway

Waveney Valley Railway

Whorlton Lido Railway

Windmill Farm Railway

Alton Towers, Staffordshire.   15 inch.

An extremely short section of dual gauge track existed at Alton Towers in the early Spring of 1979 where former *Rhyl Miniature Railway* Atlantic No.103 *John* was steamed, though it is uncertain if passengers were ever carried. The locomotive was in green livery; it moved from here to Whorlton Lido and again to Lightwater Valley near Ripon.

John was a visitor - the first Barnes ever to operate at Ravenglass during early May, 1996 and carried running No.102 on the front buffer beam. This has since been corrected to read No.103. *John* was one of six similar locomotives built by Albert Barnes of Rhyl in the early 1920's. No.103 is now in private ownership appearing occasionally at special events. In May, 1998 *John* visited the *Romney, Hythe & Dymchurch Railway*, the first Barnes to do so.

Barnes Atlantic No.103 John was at Alton Towers, a rare event perhaps to find this locomotive in steam. Note the third rail installation. 15th April, 1979.

"If the fascination engendered by locomotion at the present day is in itself so intense, the attractive powers of locomotion in miniature must of necessity be even greater still"

W. J. Bassett-Lowke. August 1911

Belle Vue Railway.   15 inch.

Zoological Gardens, Hyde Road, Manchester

The 15 inch gauge Belle Vue Railway had four differing layouts. The first was opened in 1928 in the form of a straight length of track from an entrance at Redgate Lane, a short distance from Longsight station and the LMS motive power depot (9A). This was later extended with a loop at one end, becoming a second layout.

The next one was at another site, starting from Parkside station which had two platforms and a traverser that was not always used. It was close to the Lion and Tiger house. After leaving the station the line became single, swinging away beneath a signal gantry and footbridge, passing various notable buildings towards the Great Lake, heading alongside Kirkmanshulme Lane in the general direction of Hyde Road, adjacent to the Lake Hotel. A spur trailing in on the outward journey led to the locomotive shed, a curved corrugated structure.

The lake was filled in and the railway moved yet again to what became the final layout. This was a complete circuit with one through single platform station, opening in 1964. At this time the railway became the Santa Fe Railroad, and an attempt was made to promote the atmosphere of American railroading by altering the locomotives' outline. The result was alarming and unsightly! By October, 1971 the ornamental features had been discarded and the locomotives returned to their normal appearance. The station sign above the booking office showing Santa Fe Railroad however remained until at least November, 1973.

Four Atlantics have operated at the Belle Vue Railway including two of the six Barnes locomotives from Rhyl. One, No.102 named *Railway Queen* was the first engine used and remained until the railway's demise. In 1963 she carried a green and yellow livery but by 1975 was repainted unlined blue. The other, No.101 *Joan*, arrived in 1970 from the Rhyl Miniature Railway still in RMR livery; she was the only serviceable locomotive at complete closure of the Belle Vue Railway in September, 1977. In 1936 a much travelled Bassett-Lowke Little Giant No.18 *George the Fifth* arrived from Southend, this became derelict during the 1950's but was eventually secured for preservation and is now at Carnforth.

During the war years a further Bassett-Lowke 30; (originally built for the Sand Hutton Railway) arrived at Belle Vue. This became *Prince Charles* which remained on the railway until closure of the system. Now in active preservation this engine operates occasionally at Ravenglass with her original name *Synolda*.

The whole site has now been used for redevelopment; much of it for house building and construction of the Bowling Centre near to the Lake Hotel, itself demolished during 1994. The remaining inset lengths of track were being broken out by mechanical means during clearance work in November, 1981.

Belle Vue Lake. Bassett-Lowke Atlantic **Prince Charles** *returning smokebox first having previously propelled on the outward journey during 1963. The building in the background was the Lake Hotel. (third layout).*

Prince Charles *returns from the Lake on a bright sunny afternoon in 1963, a convenient footbridge provided an interesting photographic view point. From here the line curved to the left beneath a signal gantry before entering the terminal station adjacent to the Lion and Tiger house.*

How it all looked. **Prince Charles** *brings in the empty stock; the passengers having previously alighted short of the station, a practice sometimes carried out to reduce the number of people on the platform at any one time. The building in the background was the slot palace. At this period the loco shed was inside a tunnel next to the Wolf house. August, 1969.*

Below. The fourth and final layout formed an oval which allowed continuous running . Here Barnes Atlantic No.102 **Railway Queen** *received ugly cosmetic attachments when the line became the Santa Fe Railroad. This locomotive was in red and yellow livery, September, 1969.*

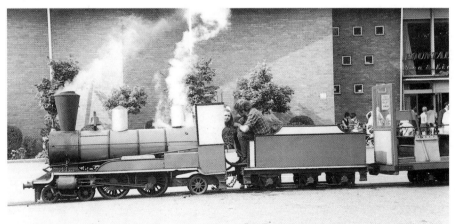

Opposite. On the third layout the station was an island platform. Here, Barnes 4-4-2 **Railway Queen** *awaits the arrival of the next train from off the single line section. The engine was then in green livery. At this time trains were propelled outwards towards the Lake in the general direction of Hyde Road. 1963.*

*In this photograph of the Belle Vue Railway system; Barnes No.102 **Railway Queen** takes a handful of passenger around the circuit; this particular section of track was the last to be removed as it was embedded in deep concrete.*

This plywood cut-out survived (showing a long frame 4-4-8) even after the period when the Belle Vue Railway was known as the Santa Fe Railroad. The Booking Office window displayed a fare card, Adults 7^1/$_2$ d, Children 5d (3p/2p!).

This 1962 photograph shows the trailing spur to the two road shed at Belle Vue on the third layout. On the right, off the picture was the Great Lake; the wall on the extreme left is Kirkmanshulme Lane. The right hand wall of the shed was approximately at a right angle facing towards Belle Vue Street. The Manchester A-Z street atlas suggests the shed site was between a snooker club and a cinema. The remainder of the railway is now buried beneath a housing site.

Blenheim Park Railway.   15 inch.

Woodstock, Oxfordshire.

This 15 inch gauge railway is situated in parkland in the grounds of Blenheim Palace. The single line followed a gradual left hand curve. It was an out and back journey with Guest Pacific No.5751 **Winston Churchill**. This engine was previously named **Prince Charles**. In earlier years it had worked on both the *Dudley Zoo Railway* and *Fairbourne Railway*. The locomotive was painted medium brown with yellow lining, the tender lettered B.P.R.

When the new railway opened during 1975 the track had not settled sufficiently, tending to be rather difficult for the locomotive to avoid slipping. Three open coaches were used. During August 0-6-0 No. 4 **Muffin** (Berwyn Engineering, 1967) was outside the running shed, it is not known if this locomotive ever worked at Blenheim Palace. Two diesel locomotives now operate the passenger service.

*At Blenheim Park Railway Guest No. 9 4-6-2 **Winston Churchill** seemed to be having difficulties! At a rather busy period this was likely a most embarrassing moment. The railway commenced at this point; the buffer stop can be seen in the background.*

Bure Valley Railway.   15 inch.

Aylsham, Norfolk.

The Bure Valley Railway officially opened on 10th July, 1990, built largely on the alignment of the former *Great Eastern Railway* line from Aylsham to Wroxham which had closed to passengers on 15th September 1952, and to all traffic on 15th June, 1983.

Aylsham is the main terminal station with good passenger facilities, and a souvenir shop. The railway has intermediate stations at Brampton, Buxton, and Coltishall. At Wroxham there is a turntable situated alongside Railtrack's north bound line from Norwich.

The nine mile long 15 inch gauge railway opened using two hired locomotives from the *Romney, Hythe & Dymchurch Railway*, 4-8-2 No.6 **Samson**, built by Davey Paxman in 1926, and 4-6-2 No.9 **Winston Churchill**, constructed in 1931 by Yorkshire Engine Company. The Bure Valley Railway obtained from Littlecote Hall No.362, Guest 2-4-2 **Sydney**, (ex-*Fairbourne Railway* **Siân**). It became No.4. This locomotive was loaned to *Cleethorpes Coast Light Railway* in 1994, moving to *Kirklees Light Railway* in May, 1998.

A 2-6-2 No.24 Sandy River & Rangely Lakes that was built at Fairbourne to 12¼ inch gauge was obtained and regauged to 15 inch to become No.2. This engine was later sold for use at the *Cleethorpes Coast Light Railway*. Another locomotive acquired was former steam outline 2-6-2T **Tracy-Jo** from the *Kirklees Light Railway*. It was rebuilt 1992 by Winson Engineering Ltd., and converted to steam power, becoming No.1, and is now a 2-6-4T named **Wroxham Broad**.

*Bure Valley Railway 2-6-4T No.1 **Wroxham Broad** pauses for a moment at Aylesham during a busy special weekend on 4th October, 1992. It may be remembered that the Redwood Valley Railway 4-6-0 No.11 **Sequoia** (illustrated under Ravenglass & Eskdale Railway) visited Aylesham on this occasion. There was another locomotive as a visitor, a 7¼ inch gauge 0-4-0 named **June** that operated within the platform limits.*

In 1994 Winson Engineering built for the Bure Valley Railway two new 'ZB' class 2-6-2s works numbers 12 and 14, becoming BVR 6 ***Blickling Hall*** and 7 ***Spitfire***. No.6 was originally finished in black but is now maroon, and No.7 is in green GWR livery. A new oil fired 2-6-2T based on a 'ZB' design, was built at Aylsham from Winson Engineering components; now No.8. A new 2-6-4T is expected to be ready for the summer season.

Another new locomotive under construction is a *Great Central Railway* ROD type 2-8-0, the first ever in 15 inch gauge. This is a ¼ scale machine and will be much smaller by comparison to the working engines. Nevertheless when completed it will be an attractive locomotive for the railway, a real scale 'standard gauge' miniature in its own right. By early Spring 1999 this locomotive was on its wheels, cylinders fitted and brake rigging prepared, the cab was already constructed. One to look out for!

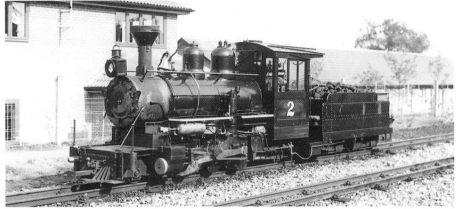

*The former Fairbourne & Barmouth Railway 2-6-2 **No.24** was photographed at the Bure Valley Railway, Aylsham as **No.2** on 4th October, 1992. The locomotive has since reverted to its original **No. 24**, and is now based at Cleethorpes.*

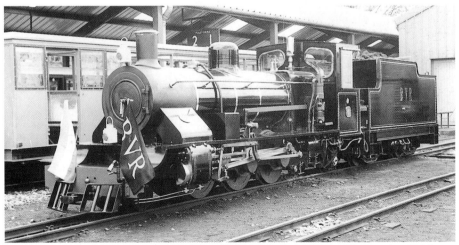

*Bure Valley ZB 2-6-2 No.6 **Blickling Hall** was built by Winson Engineering 1994 and was originally in black livery. Photographed on 29th May, 1994. (The engine was then unnamed).*

Cleethorpes Coast Light Railway.   15 inch.

Cleethorpes, Lincolnshire.   (opened in 1972 as 14¼ inch gauge)

The conversion of this railway from the unusual gauge of 14¼ inch to a more rational standard is quite an achievement.   The benefit is really enormous. The new owners of this railway completed the task of altering the gauge by the middle of 1994 and the first 15 inch gauge locomotive, albeit only on loan, was K.Hardy's 1991 built 0-4-0 No.1.

This in itself was notable but what followed later was a series of Gala events, when tremendous support was immediately forthcoming from the other private owners and established railways.

At the present time the railway starts at Lakeside station (adjacent to Kings Road). From here it passes alongside the locomotive sheds - and there is a free shuttle service to them on Gala days - then follows a long left hand curve in sight of the Humber Estuary heading towards Kingsway station. Here there is a run round loop, engines returning tender first.

There are plans in the pipeline for extensions to the system so the future of this railway long term is good. Cleethorpes has had the use of both the former Fairbourne 2-4-2's **Siân** and **Katie**, in the past. Of particular interest during 1997 was the temporary loan of (then) the only remaining 4-4-0 Cagney locomotive in the U.K. Light refreshments are available at both stations.

*Kingsway station - a triple Bassett-Lowke! The train engine is **Synolda**, pilots are **King George** and **Little Giant**! An exceedingly unusual photograph of three builds of Bassett-Lowke engines, of Classes 30, 20 and 10. The lettering on the tender of the centre locomotive indicated Whorlton Lido Railway; the Class 10 **Little Giant** was in a new maroon livery. The date of this historic event was 20th May, 1995.*

Cleethorpes Coast Light Railway, after conversion to fifteen inch gauge, borrowed 0-4-0 No.1 for their early steam services. The photograph shows this interesting engine at Lakeside station on 24th July, 1994.

Brooks Railroad Cagney 4-4-0 No.2 visited Cleethorpes albeit as a static exhibit; and for the first time in 25 years left its home at Strumpshaw Hall. It was (then) the only known example of these once numerous locomotives in Britain. 27th September, 1997.

This 2-6-2 built at Fairbourne in 1990 to 12¼ inch gauge as No.24 was re-gauged to 15 inch. It then worked on both the Bure Valley Railway and the Kirklees Light Railway as No.2 visiting Cleethorpes on 30th September, 1995. This photograph shows the locomotive working a passenger train from Lakeside to Kingsway. No.2 was later purchased for use at Cleethorpes as No.24.

Dreamland Narrow Gauge Steam Railway.
15 inch.   Margate, Kent.

In August, 1974 the Dreamland Miniature Railway was operating with steam using former Rhyl Barnes 4-4-2 No.104 *Billie*. The railway extended about ¼ mile from the station, the line passing behind various buildings; a scenic railway and terminating on waste ground. The train propelled back to the two platform station, unusual in having a traverser. A Bassett-Lowke 4-4-2 No. 15 *Prince Edward of Wales* was here until 1967. The Railway closed in 1979.

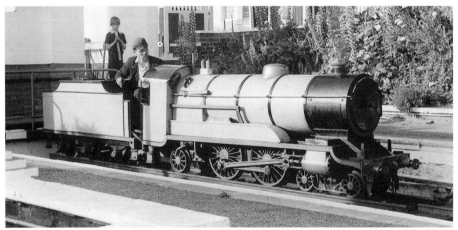

*It seemed quite unusual to find one of the six Barnes Atlantics in Margate. On this occasion No. 104 **Billie** was in use; it had been running without the splashers but the helpful driver replaced them for this photograph! August, 1974.*

Dudley Zoo Railway.   15 inch.
West Midlands.

When looking back into the history of Dudley Zoo it seems that almost every locomotive of between 10¼ and 15 inch gauges has been at Dudley Zoo in one form or another! Dudley operated pre-war with a 10¼ inch gauge railway from 1938 and by 1947 had been rebuilt as a 15 inch system. Various locomotives have been used over the years; this information being already well documented elsewhere.

During August, 1982 two of the former Barnes Atlantics were available for traffic, No. 105 *Michael* was inside the shed and No.104 *Billie* (without name plates) worked the shuttle service propelling outwards along the single line. A chalked board indicated the 800 metre journey into the woods was 30p return. Even in August passengers were minimal. *Billie* had formally worked at Dreamland, Margate during August, 1974. Both engines returned to Rhyl during 1984. Dudley Zoo Railway finally closed in September, 1992, and the track was afterwards lifted.

Above: Considering the number of locomotives that had worked on the Dudley Zoo Railway over the years not as many photographs exist as one might imagine; perhaps it was a line that not many enthusiasts visited. Here, Barnes Atlantic No. 104 **Billie** is blowing off at Dudley Zoo station in August, 1982.

Left: **Billie** gives a rapid burst of speed towards the camera on the Dudley Zoo line one August afternoon in 1982.

Near the extremity of the Dudley Zoo Railway in August, 1982. The single line passed through the perimeter gates of the site for a short distance; closing them at the end of the day was a duty the driver. During this period, **No. 104**, then unmistakable with its cast cab side number plates, ran without its name plates.

East Lancashire Railway.   15 inch.

former electric traction workshops, Bury.

A 15 inch demonstration line was installed at Bury in the yard outside the standard gauge shed, where the former *British Railways* electric multiple units that worked between Bury and Manchester Victoria were serviced. It was a third rail system replaced when Manchester's *Metrolink* came on stream.

The miniature line itself used a third rail on the standard gauge, allowing limited working for about 100 yards; motive power was a 4-6-2 No. 5751 **Prince William** ex-Carnforth, built by Guest Engineering No.9 in 1949. The stock was a former 1984 Liverpool International Garden Festival coach.

*Pacific No. 5751 **Prince William** keeping company at Bury with a pair of Class 5's Nos. 5407 and 45337. The tender letters SMR, now removed, indicated the Pacific's previous home at Steamtown Miniature Railway at Carnforth. 25th February 1996.*

*Opposite: The flagship at Fairbourne was Bassett-Lowke Class 30 Atlantic 32 **Count Louis**, which was always well cared for. This photograph of August, 1975 shows the locomotive is pristine condition close to the station site. There is still hope for full restoration of this engine in due course.*

Fairbourne Railway.   15 inch.

Beach Road, Fairbourne, Merionethshire.

At first Fairbourne had a 2ft. gauge tramway worked by horses; the tramway did carry passengers but it stopped short of the Ferry. In 1916 the fifteen inch gauge Fairbourne Railway was opened to traffic; their first locomotive was a Class 20 Bassett-Lowke Atlantic No.22 named **Prince Edward of Wales**, built the previous year. This locomotive left Fairbourne in 1923 for Southport and the next Bassett-Lowke Atlantic to arrive in 1925 was Class 30 No.32 **Count Louis** built in 1924. This locomotive spent the greater part of its working life at Fairbourne, and for a few months, after the sale in 1984 of the 15 inch gauge railway, was on display inside the Booking Office. Though now saved, but no longer at Fairbourne, it awaits funding and a full rebuild.

In 1927 a third rail was laid to accommodate an 18 inch. gauge Great Northern Single No.1; built by the Regent Street Polytechnic, London, to a Bagnall design of 1893, staying a few years before being sold. In 1923 0-4-0T Heywood built **Katie** was bought from Southport. **Katie**, an original Heywood engine of 1896, was dismantled at Fairbourne some three years later and more recently the surviving parts subsequently went to Ravenglass where rebuilding her has already commenced.

The 15 inch gauge railway operated over $1^3/4$ miles from Fairbourne to Penrhyn Point. Here it made connection with the Barmouth ferryboats, sometimes for the passengers a rather choppy sail across the Mawddach estuary! An old established custom is to fly the flag at the ferry to indicate when the railway is operating; something that is still done to day.

A number of engines have worked on the Fairbourne Railway, including a 4-6-0 built by G&S Light Engineering (No.9) of 1949 No. 5751 **Prince Charles**, and (No.10) from the same

builder in 1950, 4-6-2 No. 57512 **Ernest W.Twining**. Two other locomotives that became the backbone of the railway's motive power were the 2-4-2's **Katie** and **Siân**. Both were built by Guest Engineering in 1956 and 1963, coming to the Fairbourne Railway in 1965 and 1963 respectively. Fairbourne also operated various internal combustion units, **Whippit Quick, Gwril, Dingo, Sylvia, Rachel** and **Tracy-Jo,** the latter a steam outline petrol/mechanical 2-6-2T, was converted by Winson Engineering in 1992 to a steam 2-6-4T; and now based on the *Bure Valley Railway*, renamed No.1 **Wroxham Broad.**

Prince Charles was rebuilt to a Pacific in 1968. This locomotive is now **Prince William** at the *Windmill Farm Railway* in West Lancashire. **Ernest W.Twining** was exported in 1987 to the Natural Garden of Shuzenji at Niji-No-Sato, Japan, arriving there on the 19th August that year to work on the *Shuzenji Railway* which opened on 1st April 1990. This locomotive ran tests after a full overhaul using a third rail on the *O-IGAWA Railway* at the town of Kanaya, Shizuoka, Japan on 30th October 1989.

The Fairbourne Railway was sold to Mr.J.Ellerton in 1984 who reconstructed the railway in 1986 to a gauge of 12¼ inch. (See appropriate section under 12¼ inch gauge railways).

Photographed at Penrhyn Point in superb lighting at the end of the day's work in 1962 is Guest Pacific 57512 **Ernest W.Twining** *in its original condition with the small cab and six wheel tender. .*

Ernest W.Twining *simply became known by its name on rebuilding to its present form. The main differences are easy to identify, the larger cab, and the new eight wheel tender. Photographed at Penrhyn Point in July, 1971. This locomotive was sold and is now back in service in Japan; it was in steam on the Shuzenji Railway at Niji-No-Sato on 21st February, 1990. (See text for further comments)*

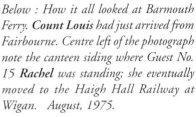

Below : How it all looked at Barmouth Ferry. **Count Louis** had just arrived from Fairbourne. Centre left of the photograph note the canteen siding where Guest No. 15 **Rachel** was standing; she eventually moved to the Haigh Hall Railway at Wigan. August, 1975.

Above: The Fairbourne Sea Train operated for one season. Former **Siân** became No. 362 **Sydney**, seen here heading towards Penrhyn Point on 27th August, 1984.

The other remaining Fairbourne 2-4-2 was left in her original condition, this was **Katie**, she was renamed **Shôn** by the new Fairbourne Railway owners. This view shows **Shôn** passing Penrhyn Halt on 27th August, 1984. The covered coach was lettered Sea Train. When disposed of **Katie** moved to Wigan in Lancashire, and from there to Cleethorpes. For a while the two sisters were reunited on the East Coast.

A picturesque late afternoon, the silence is broken by **Ernest W. Twining** emerging from the shadows of the dunes. Very soon all will change as excited passengers make their way to the ferry boat. July 1971.

1990 National Garden Festival. 15 inch.

Gateshead, Tyne & Wear.

The National Garden Festival's total area of some 200 acres was spread out over four sites giving an end to end length of about 1½ miles. It opened to the public from 18th May, 1990, until 21st October the same year. The northern and southern pairs of sites were joined by a 500 yard corridor (The Boulevard) served by a conventional electric tramway on which travel was free. Like the Liverpool International Garden Festival of 1984, Gateshead had a 15 inch gauge miniature railway. The railway was just over a mile in length, with two stations, and connected the two northern sites, Riverside (where the rolling stock was housed) and Dunston. Fares were 50p single/£1 return (unlike Liverpool which was free), the line following a dumb-bell shaped course. The two loops were linked by a short section of single track across a Bailey bridge over a road and the River Team, with a steep climb to the bridge in each direction. Two train sets were used.

Motive power was hired from the *Ravenglass and Eskdale Railway* and *Romney, Hythe & Dymchurch Railway*. At the time only a diesel, No.12 ***John Southland***, could be spared from New Romney as some of their locomotives were elsewhere, but the Ravenglass & Eskdale provided two steam engines, 0-8-2 ***River Irt*** and 2-6-2 ***Northern Rock*** The R&ER also provided a diesel, ***Shelagh of Eskdale***, and a battery locomotive used during the line's construction.

When the Festival closed three coaches were converted to accommodate wheel chairs and were sold to the Natural Garden of Shuzenji at Niji-No-Sato in Japan, to be used on the 15 inch gauge system which had opened on 1st April, 1990.

A view at the Gateshead National Garden Festival showing Ravenglass & Eskdale Railway ***River Irt*** *on the final curve before reaching Riverside station. In the far distance is the basin and staiths leading to the River Tyne. Almost above the last coach of the train is* ***Locomotion****, a replica engine built for the 1975 Rail 150 celebrations on loan from Beamish North of England Museum. 28th June, 1990.*

*Here **Northern Rock**, another locomotive from Ravenglass, waits to depart from Dunston station, Gateshead on 6th July, 1990. Behind the trees at a higher level was the electric tramway with cars representing Blackpool, London, Newcastle and Sheffield systems.*

Goshen Fields, Bury Fiesta. 15 inch.
Bury, Lancashire.

This was a temporary line on the south side of Bury which operated for a few days during the second week of August, 1979 using Bassett-Lowke Atlantic No. 18 ***George the Fifth*** loaned on this occasion from Carnforth. The track, about 200yds in length, was laid alongside the fence of the field then veered to the left along a gradual curve. It was a typical push/pull run propelling tender first on the outward trip. Few photographs exist of this event.

*A temporary railway at Goshen Fields, near Bury. Here, Bassett-Lowke Atlantic No. 18 **George the Fifth** worked this site for a few days at Bury Fiesta. 12th August, 1979.*

Haigh Hall Railway.   15 inch.

Haigh Hall Country Park, Wigan, Lancashire.

Haigh Hall Railway opened in July, 1986. The park is owned by Wigan Metropolitan Council. An idea had been floated to install a railway from the Hall to the Leeds & Liverpool canal but the cost, due to engineering considerations, would have been prohibitive. The present layout was operated initially with diesel power at a fare of 30p; standard roll tickets were issued but they are not special prints for the railway. The railway passes through woodland for much of its length, initially serving two stations. The terminal station at Haigh Hall South was intended for two train operation having a passing loop. There is a large stock shed to house the locomotives and other rolling stock.

The official opening of the 15 inch railway was carried out by Mrs Joy Smith, wife of Wigan Metro Finance Committee Chairman on 23rd August, 1986. The special train was steam hauled using former *Fairbourne Railway* **Katie**, (2-4-2 G&S Engineering 14/1956) .

The event was marked by much flag waving, along with the attendance of a brass band, before conveying the official guests on a ceremonial journey of the circuit. Since the railway was opened the track has been extended on the south east side, through the upper plantations, and a section of the original line taken out. Operation of the railway is unadvertised but it is sometimes open at weekends and daily during the summer. **Katie** was re-named **Haigh Hall**, a name she took later to the *Cleethorpes Coast Light Railway*; GWR type side plates were fitted as No. 7204 (a number chosen at random by school children). There are two diesel locomotives, the ex-*Fairbourne Railway* **Rachel** and an Alan Keef diesel; No.41 new in 1992 (now unnamed) operates the service trains. The platform at Haigh Hall North ceased to be used at an unspecified date.

The official opening day at Haigh Hall, Wigan. After the various celebrations had taken place with the accompaniment of a female dancer and the support of the Red Rose band, the civic party made a tour of the railway behind the former **Katie**.

Just clear of the station the Haigh Hall Railway climbs up towards the plantations. **Haigh Hall** *had been cleaned and well prepared for the day's work ahead. Note the name plate in the normal position; at a later date curved plates were evident. The head board is The Lancastrian.*

Kirklees Light Railway.   15 inch.

Clayton West, Yorkshire.

The opening of a new railway, especially when it is built to 15 inch gauge, is always an exciting event. The Kirklees Light Railway, based at Clayton West, is located at the end of the former BR (originally L&YR) branch that closed in January, 1983 and which connected with the existing Huddersfield-Penistone line. KLR public services began on 19th October, 1991. Trains ran at weekends as far as a new halt at Cuckoo's Nest, on the north side of the line about a mile from Clayton West, where a run round was installed. This halt is in open countryside with a footpath leading to the surrounding area.

The main terminus to the west of the former BR station has a spacious layout with three platform faces, water column and turntable. Nearby is the locomotive shed which houses the line's steam engines designed and built by Mr. Brian Taylor.

Fox is a red 2-6-2 Side Tank built during 1987, **Badger** a green 0-6-4ST completed in 1991 and diesel **Jay** was built in the workshops in 1992. The locomotive names were selected from wild life seen in the vicinity of the railway during reconstruction.

In 1993 a 2-6-2, originally built as No.24 at Fairbourne to $12^{1}/_{4}$ inch gauge, arrived at Clayton West via the *Bure Valley Railway*. This locomotive had been regauged to 15 inch, entered service as No.2 on the KLR and was repainted yellow. This engine visited the Cleethorpes line for their Gala event of 18-19th May, 1996, being later purchased for use on that railway from the *Bure Valley Railway,* again No.24 on returning to black livery. Coaching stock was originally varnished teak but due to the effects of the elements has now been painted red. Steam heating and electric lighting are now standard on all passenger vehicles.

By Boxing Day 1992 the railway had reached Skelmanthorpe station, services being extended from Cuckoo's Nest. The final extension, passing through a deep rock cutting and Shelley Woodhouse tunnel, (511 yards long) enabled the railway to reach Shelley where run round facilities and a turntable were constructed. The platform is only a short distance from the site of Clayton West Junction. The full line became open from 31st May, 1997.

In the following Spring a new refreshment room opened at Clayton West. Inside the building on static display is a 7¼ inch gauge American 4-4-0 No.44 named *Jersey City*. In early 1998, a Kitson Meyer 0-4+4-0T named *Hawk* and in blue was completed and entered service. 2-4-2 *Siân* came to the railway in May, 1998. There are good free parking and passenger facilities at Clayton West.

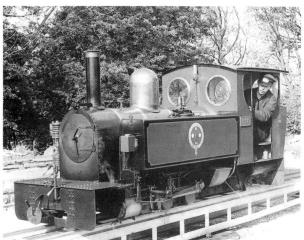

Kirklees Light Railway 2-6-2T Fox along with Badger have been regular engines on this railway until overhaul became due for the 2-6-2T in 1998. On the turntable at Clayton West is Fox, a 1987 build by B. Taylor. The smart red livery is very eye catching, and the choice of name original! 3rd May, 1993.

Approaching Shelley is 0-4-0 + 0-4-0 Kitson Meyer **Hawk**, *the very latest engine from B. Taylor. This very smart addition to the Kirklees stock carries a blue livery with the railway's crest on the side tanks, note the rear exhaust stack! On the extreme left of the picture is the Emley Moor television transmission mast serving parts of Yorkshire.*

Opposite: At Shelley station before the erection of the passenger shelter. Here, 0-6-4ST **Badger** *has just arrived with the 11.am train from Clayton West on 6th July, 1997. Forward from the train is a turntable giving access to the run-round loop, on the left, used by each train engine after turning. Note a headlight is now fitted for use through the long tunnel. At the present time there is no passenger connection with the standard gauge Huddersfield-Penistone line.*

Lakeside Miniature Railway.   15 inch.

Southport, Lancashire.

Lakeside Miniature Railway is located at Marine Drive, adjacent to the lake. Historically the railway is of great interest; it opened at 3 pm. on 25th May, 1911. It was then known as The *Llewelyn Miniature Railway Ltd.*, and still to this day uses the same initials! Several well known locomotives worked on this relatively short railway including Heywood 0-4-0T *Katie* built in 1896, which was here from 1919 to 1923, and a Bassett-Lowke Class 20, 4-4-2 No.22, *Prince Edward of Wales* arrived from the *Fairbourne Railway* in 1923.

At the present time there are two stations, Pleasureland (close to the amusement site) with its island platform, booking office and shelter, adjacent to where the locomotive shed and repair shop is to be found, and Marine Parade at the north end of the line. Here there are two platforms with independent run round loops. The station is unmanned and the area around it is now expected to be eventually redeveloped.

The LMR single line is straight from Pleasureland for about a ¼ mile passing beneath the now closed Pier Railway, under a bridge where there is a sharp left hand curve towards Marine Parade station. Some cosmetic signals exist alongside the railway.

On 27th March, 1983 a steam Gala was held at Southport when visiting engines operated; these were Bassett-Lowke Atlantics No. 18, *George the Fifth*, No. 22 *Princess Elizabeth*, (from Carnforth) and Class 30 *Synolda* (Ravenglass). At the present time one rebuilt Bassett-Lowke 4-4-2 No.15 *Red Dragon*, now magnificently reincarnated, is based at Southport. It is used occasionally, though unadvertised, on off peak Saturday afternoons working alternate trains weather permitting. This engine is in the LMR bright red livery, and is sometimes displayed outside the running shed when not in use. A number of diesel locomotives work the normal passenger service.

A rare shed view of Southport's Lakeside Miniature Railway. Left to right, Bassett-Lowke No. 22 Princess Elizabeth, B-L No. 18 George the Fifth, and B-L No. 30 Synolda. This was a special event weekend, so far not repeated.
27th March, 1983.

Marine Parade station is the end of the line. Just arrived from Pleasureland is a double headed steam special worked by Bassett-Lowke No. 22 **Princess Elizabeth** *and piloted by Bassett-Lowke No. 30* **Synolda**. *27th March, 1983.*

Left: The interesting Booking Office building at Pleasureland station, photographed out of season, 5th October, 1991.

Below: A view of Lakeside Miniature Railway's outer terminal station at Marine Parade on a windy afternoon, 5th October, 1991. Note the illustration on the far left showing a Barlow locomotive; the fares at this time were 50p single, 80p return.

*Southport's own 4-4-2 **Red Dragon** arrives at Marine Parade station, running in between the service train as required. 26th September 1996.*

*A general view of Southport's Pleasureland station looking North - note two-train operation; on the right is 1991 built Atlantic **Red Dragon**, having just arrived with a train from Marine Parade. On the far left is a triple articulated twin set, still identified as FTO Rly., a reminder of those far off days of 1951 and the Far Tottering & Oystercreek Railway, a 15 inch gauge railway built at Battersea Park contemporary with the Festival of Britain. 19th September, 1998.*

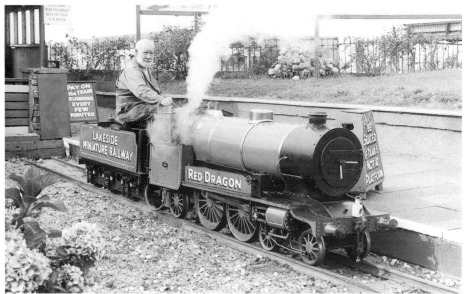

The end of the line at Marine Parade station. The occasional Saturday steaming of No.15 **Red Dragon** *has proved popular. The Atlantic had just reversed having worked tender first from Pleasureland station, and is about to run round the stock. It is proposed that the large area outside the station will be redeveloped in the near future and site clearance work was in progress during May, 1999.   The LMR will probably be in the centre of this new complex.   19th September, 1998.*

An early post war view of Bassett-Lowke Atlantic **King George**, *seen here at Marine Parade station on 2nd June 1951. Note the dress of the day and the odd bowler hat.*

Photograph: Neville Fields

Lappa Valley Railway.   15 inch.

St. Newlyn East, Newquay, Cornwall.

The Lappa Valley Railway was built on part of the track bed of the former *Great Western Railway* branch line from Newquay to Chacewater which closed on 4th February, 1963, a Beeching casualty at that time. The new 15 inch gauge railway was constructed along a one mile section of this line from Benny Halt to East Wheal Rose opening in June, 1974.

The railway has two steam locomotives, 0-6-4T (rebuilt from a 0-6-2T in 1990) No.1 *Zebedee* Severn Lamb No.34 of 1974 which was built for the line and a 0-6-0 No.4 *Muffin*, Berwyn Engineering of 1967, ex-*Longleat Light Railway*. At East Wheal Rose there is also a 10¼ inch gauge line with a diesel locomotive, and a 7¼ inch with a petrol. This area has been landscaped offering family attractions.

Lightwater Valley Miniature Railway. 15 inch.

Near Ripon, North Yorkshire.

The 15 inch gauge railway at Lightwater Valley is about ¾ mile in length; a long single line continuous formation with a trailing spur into the shed and workshops of the line. Trains work in a clockwise rotation calling at halts en route.

The locomotives are housed inside a shed that is normally open to visitors to the complex. The resident locomotive is a Severn Lamb s/o 2-8-0DH. At the time of writing 4-4-0 *Yvette* (built 1946) and 4-4-2 Bassett Lowke No.10 *Little Giant* (dating back to 1905) share this accommodation. The world's oldest working internal combustion engine, 4-4-4T *Blacolvesley,* built in 1909 by Bassett-Lowke and new to Blakesley Hall as No.3, was stored (as LNER 1326) at Lightwater Valley. This unique locomotive has since moved to the *Ravenglass & Eskdale Railway*. One of the former Rhyl Barnes Atlantics No.103 *John* was stored here; occasionally this engine also visits Ravenglass.

The Carland Scot, the only known one built in 15 inch gauge, has moved to Cleethorpes; 6100 *Royal Scot* was once diesel electric powered. It was restored to steam operation and did work normal service trains at Lightwater Valley. No.10 *Little Giant* is now in private ownership but can still be seen occasionally as a visitor at other locations. An entrance fee is levied at this site.

Opposite: 4-4-0 No.111 Yvette pilots Rio Grande 2-8-0 No.278 around the Lightwater Valley circuit during the late afternoon of 16th August, 1982.

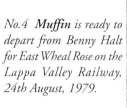

No.4 **Muffin** is ready to depart from Benny Halt for East Wheal Rose on the Lappa Valley Railway, 24th August, 1979.

The only 15 inch gauge **Carland Scot**, 6100 here unnamed, with Arthur Butler on the footplate, ex-British Railways driver. At Lightwater Valley, 16th July, 1989.

Liverpool International Garden Festival.

15 inch.   1984.

The Liverpool International Garden Festival was opened by HM The Queen on 2nd May, 1984. Built by the Merseyside Development Corporation it was the first International Garden Festival in Britain, remaining open until 14th October, 1984.

A 15 inch gauge railway was constructed by contractors to serve the 125 acre site adjacent to the River Mersey and motive power was hired from existing operators.

The new line was 2¹/₂ miles in length with six stations; these were located at Fulwood, The Mill, Festival Hall, Dingle and Herculaneum. Both the latter bore station names of the former Liverpool Overhead Railway.

Festival Hall was a magnificent station that would have lasted for many years. Here a trailing branch, unusual on a 15 inch gauge system, entered the circuit from Herculaneum. This section was usually operated by **Silver Jubilee**, a *Ravenglass & Eskdale Railway* diesel multiple unit, conveying passengers from the Herculaneum entrance. (The other one was at Fulwood). A station existed on the branch at Play Centre close to Festival Hall station. Here passengers from Herculaneum had to cross by a footbridge to Festival Hall if they wished to continue by rail. The reason was to allow the DMU to operate without conflicting with the main line trains.

All the stations had substantial buildings; the track, steeply graded in places, was a continuous

*Romney, Hythe & Dymchurch Krupp Pacific **Black Prince** about to enter Festival Hall station with a train from Fulwood and The Mill. The pelican to the left of the picture was constructed by artist David Petersen; with a wing span of 14 feet the weight of it was over a ton. In more recent years **Black Prince** has been rebuilt with a higher running plate. 14th May, 1984.*

circuit with two large loops joined in the centre by a double line section and all controlled by colour light signalling. A trailing spur served the locomotive shed and access to the stock sidings where locomotives could be changed over. The railway had many manned foot crossings controlling pedestrian movements when trains were operating. As might be anticipated there were large queues of intending passengers as rail travel was free. Special signs indicated a likely 45 minute waiting period at some stations!

All passengers had to alight at Festival Hall and rejoin another queue if they wished to proceed further. The station work was extremely slow and a journey around the full circuit could be a tiresome time consuming task. Despite the shortcomings of the system the journey was very popular and it gave excellent views of the many gardens en route. The railway operated in a clockwise direction and trains passed each other on the double line section.

Motive power for the festival was provided by the two leading 15 inch gauge railways. *Ravenglass & Eskdale Railway* loaned their 0-8-2 **River Irt** and the diesel **Shelagh of Eskdale**. The *Romney, Hythe & Dymchurch Railway* also supplied on hire 0-4-0 No.4 **The Bug**, 4-8-2 No.6 **Samson** (repainted red at the request of the festival management due to the Liverpool football connection!) and No.11 **Black Prince** (Krupp) then in original condition. The R.H.D.R provided five teak coaches along with their Royal Saloon. 18 custom built coaches were constructed at Carnforth. The Liverpool Garden Festival was said to have cost in excess of £19.3M. After Liverpool there were other garden festivals at Stoke and Glasgow but only Gateshead had a 15 inch gauge railway.

*Romney, Hythe & Dymchurch Railway 4-8-2 **Samson** with a train at Festival Hall, the largest station on the railway. To the right (off the picture) was the branch platform where the diesel multiple unit made a connection with the main line service. At the top right of the photograph can be seen a viewing point which allowed visitors a panoramic view of the River Mersey. 14th May, 1984.*

*Just beyond the running shed and adjacent to the BBC Children's Exhibition a convenient footbridge had been erected which allowed photography of trains on the climb towards Dingle. Against the Liverpool skyline is Ravenglass & Eskdale Railway 0-8-2 **River Irt** slowing for a signal check ahead. 14th May, 1984.*

Littlecote Riverside Railway.   15 inch.

Littlecote Hall, near Hungerford.

The railway at Littlecote Hall was about ¹/₂ mile in length with a wide loop at each end of the single line. The shed is situated close to the property where their steam locomotive was housed. The railway served a purpose providing a link between the car park and the hall. The 2-4-2 (Guest 18/1963) came from the *Fairbourne Railway* as No.362 (the Fairbourne telephone number!) **Sydney**, a rebuild of **Siân**, and had operated the FR's *Sea Train* during the final 15 inch gauge season in 1984.

No.362 had been cosmetically renovated with red edges to the footplating and boiler bands, the head light had likewise received red numerals. The massive cab side numerals used at Fairbourne gave way to something nearer in proportion albeit red on black. On closure of the Littlecote line in 1991 the locomotive moved to the *Bure Valley Railway* to become their No.4. The ongoing history has been well documented, the engine visiting the *Ravenglass & Eskdale Railway* and *Cleethorpes Coast Light Railway* sites, and now looking more like her original *Fairbourne Railway* condition due to dedicated restoration.

*The immaculate No. 362 **Sydney** waits beneath the trees at Littlecote Hall at the car park end of the line. 26th July, 1986.*

Longleat Railway.   15 inch.

Warminster, Wiltshire.

The railway is located at Longleat House. It is about a mile long through the grounds and has one steam locomotive 0-6-2T No.3 **Dougal** built in 1970 by Severn Lamb and two diesel units. Bassett-Lowke Little Giant 4-4-2 No.18 **George the Fifth** was at Longleat from 1977 until early 1979. Whilst there it was re-named (with the same name) during October, 1978, by Mrs Elenora Steel, daughter of Henry Greenly. This engine had been recovered by dedicated enthusiasts from the *Belle Vue Railway*, Manchester fourteen years earlier.

*Photographed outside the shed in August, 1977, is Longleat Railway's own steam locomotive 0-6-2T No. 3 **Dougal**,   Inside the shed was Bassett-Lowke 4-4-2 No. 18 **George the Fifth**, a visitor to the line.*

Markeaton Park Light Railway.   15 inch.

Derby.   (access via A5111 Ring Road).

The original railway in the park began with a petrol engine in 1989; it operated for a half mile using two open coaches from a station adjacent to the car park. By 1995 a new operator expressed interest and the railway was extended from its former terminus to a new station at Mundy Halt, the station taking its name from the Mundy family who owned the estate for over 400 years. This new station is close to the Mundy Play Centre. Maria Georgina Mundy made a gift of this land to the Town of Derby in 1903.

The new line is almost a mile in length, crossing two bridges en route with a passing loop for two train operation and run round facilities at both stations. The line was passed for passenger use by HM Railway Inspectorate on 24th September, 1996; and trains operated later that month. The steam locomotive is an 0-4-2T built by Exmoor Steam Railway (works No.300 of 7/96) named **Markeaton Lady** and finished in blue with yellow lining.

The initial services operated with two custom built coaches, adapted for wheelchair passengers, both built at Exmoor. The coaching stock is painted red. The locomotive is housed in an extensive shed adjacent to the large car park; services operating every weekend and daily from Easter. Initial steam service commenced on 28th September, followed by the railway's official opening by Councillor Martin Repton, Chair of Derby City Leisure Services Committee, on 24th October, 1996. The railway also has three diesel locomotives. An interesting railway with good photographic viewpoints. A third coach has now been obtained.

*The first train of the day arrives at Mundy Halt on 21st October, 1996. The locomotive is **Markeaton Lady**. At this time only two coaches were available for traffic, the other was awaiting delivery from the manufacturer.*

Paradise Railway.   15 inch.

Paradise Park, Hayle, Cornwall.

There were three miniature railways very close together, Paradise Railway being one of them; the others were *Age of Steam* and the *Towans Railway*. The Paradise Railway was opened during 1976 using two diesel locomotives. It is about ¼ mile in length laid with heavy weight track which formed a circuit around a large house. Passengers were taken round twice at quite high speed!

Only one steam locomotive was evident, a 0-4-0 named **Chough**, built by Williem Van der Heiden in 1968. The locomotive had been in store in a garage in London in 1970 and arrived for trials at New Romney in July without nameplates. She was known as **Tekkel** (Dutch for a small dog with short legs), and moved on in January, 1973 to a farm at Acrise in Kent; noted there 8/1977, then to Hayle in August, 1978 with **Tekkel** plates but soon re-named **Chough.**

Paradise Railway was operating **Chough** during August 1979. This locomotive has moved around more than most others and was at Banff on the *Great North of Scotland* trackbed during 1984 until 1986. It also worked in Suffolk and West Wales before being purchased for a line at Whitworth Hall, but it did not stay there very long and emigrated in 1996 to a new railway at Bear Creek Park, near Vancouver, Canada. A similar locomotive, **Sarah-Kate**, is at the *Bush Mill Railway*, Port Arthur, Tasmania. The Paradise Railway still operates using diesel power.

Chough pauses for a few minutes during the afternoon's busy running schedule. Surprisingly this locomotive had quite a turn of speed. 22nd August, 1979.

Rail 150   15 inch.

Stockton & Darlington Celebrations, Shildon.

A short 15 inch gauge line was installed at Shildon in August 1975 as part of the 150th anniversary celebrations of the opening of the *Stockton & Darlington Railway*. In steam was Bassett-Lowke Class 20 No.22, an Atlantic ex-*Lakeside Miniature Railway,* Southport, fresh from restoration in blue livery lined out in red. Passenger rides were provided, outward smokebox first; propelled on return. In the open was Bassett-Lowke Class 30 No.32 4-4-2 **Count Louis**, built in 1924, from the 15 inch gauge *Fairbourne Railway* and the partially constructed 2-6-2 **Northern Rock** - now a well known and powerful locomotive of the *Ravenglass & Eskdale Railway* in Cumbria.

Undercover miniature exhibits on display were $7^{1}/_{4}$ inch gauge Garratt 4-8-2+2-8-4 No.5928 **Mount Kilimanjaro**, in *East African Railways* livery and oil fired, built by Coleby Simkins 4/1973, and two locomotives from the $10^{1}/_{4}$ inch gauge *Stapleford Park Miniature Railway.* They were the superb 2-8-4 Berkshire No.752 (then named **The Lady Margaret**) and LMS 5X Jubilee 4-6-0 No. 5565 **Victoria.**

Another locomotive which was on display was the late Brian Nicholson's $10^{1}/_{4}$ inch gauge Leek & Manifold 2-6-4T **E.R.Calthrop**, built by Coleby Simkins for a new railway which later opened at Rudyard Lake, near Leek in Staffordshire, (now closed). The L&M 2-6-4T then moved to Kessingland, and afterwards to Trago Mills near Liverton.

Mount Kilimanjaro operated on the now closed steeply graded *Croesor Junction & Pacific Railway,* a private line in a remote part of North Wales. It was stored for a short time at the *Conwy Valley Railway* Museum site during 1994, overhauled by R.B.Rogers, converted to coal firing and was operated occasionally at *Weston Park Railway*. The two Stapleford engines are operational again, but the nameplates are now removed from the Berkshire 752.

The temporary railway at Shildon utilised an ex-Lakeside Miniature Railway Bassett-Lowke Class 20 Atlantic No. 22, running without number or name. August, 1975.

Complementary with the Stockton & Darlington Railway 1550 celebrations in 1975 was an outdoor display at Darlington where the 15 inch gauge Bassett-Lowke 4-4-2T **Blacolvesley,** *an internal combustion locomotive now with an 8h.p. Austin engine) of 1909 was exhibited along with the 15 inch gauge* **Little Titan** *breakdown crane. It is quite remarkable that this unique locomotive has survived. At Darlington, its livery was unlined black, quite different from how it is today, now restored externally to what is now believed to be as near as possible to the original finish along with a beautiful scroll displaying her name.*

From her NER appearance, **Blacolvesley** *was later cosmetically restored as LNER 1326 and, by August 1982, could be seen at the Lightwater Valley Railway near Ripon. She is now in the ownership of Dr. Bob Tebb and further mechanical restoration work is contemplated; very likely it may be possible to return this elderly Bassett-Lowke lady to active service.*

Ravenglass & Eskdale Railway.   15 inch.

Ravenglass, Cumbria.

The first railway at Ravenglass served a mining area at Eskdale; it was built to 3ft. gauge, and was worked by Manning Wardle 0-6-0T's. The line opened to traffic in 1875; lasting until around 1913. Soon Bassett-Lowke took an interest in the site; by 1915 the first fifteen inch gauge train worked the initial mile to Muncaster. The remainder reopened progressively until the full line was available two years later. Motive power were early Bassett-Lowke locomotives and Heywood tank engines.

In 1960 the railway entered preservation; possibly spurred on by a similar venture in Wales when the Narrow Gauge *Talyllyn Railway* was taken over some years previously. The Ravenglass & Eskdale Railway is situated in one of the most beautiful areas of England. The seven mile journey from Ravenglass to the terminal station at Dalegarth has intermediate stations at Muncaster Mill, Irton Road, The Green and Beckfoot, with a halt at Fisherground, between the latter two.

The present steam locomotives are 2-8-2 **River Esk**, built by Davey Paxman in 1923, 0-8-2 **River Irt**, R&ER of 1928, a rebuild of Heywood **Muriel** of 1894 and a 2-8-2 **River Mite** constructed by Clarkson, of York, 1966. The three locomotives were named after the rivers around Ravenglass.

A 2-6-2 **Northern Rock** was built in 1976 in the railway's workshop - this locomotive was displayed partly built at 'Rail 150' during the celebrations at Shildon in 1975. Kerr Stuart **Bonnie Dundee** came to Ravenglass as a 2ft. narrow gauge 0-4-2WT dating back to 1901, originating from the Dundee Gas Works. Rebuilding was carried out and it emerged as No.11, an 0-4-2T in 1981, retaining her name. In 1996 the side tanks were removed, rebuilding her to an 0-4-2 tender engine.

*An early view of Ravenglass & Eskdale Railway No.3 **River Irt** at Ravenglass station, 5th September, 1968. During rebuilding in 1928 some features of **Muriel** were retained.*

The diminutive vertical boiler locomotive **Flower of the Forest** built at Ravenglass in 1985 only appears on special occasions having limited pulling power; it does however work along the main line as far as Muncaster Mill. Bassett-Lowke Class 30 4-4-2 **Synolda** of 1912, which spent many years at *Belle Vue Railway*, Manchester, is normally housed in the railway's museum. Being a useful locomotive, she sees periodic use on special event days when an intensive service is operated.

The only Bassett-Lowke 4-4-4T **Blacolvesley** of 1909, a unique petrol/mechanical locomotive has joined the railway after considerable restoration work was carried out. Work is progressing on rebuilding the former *Eaton Hall Railway* Heywood 0-4-0T **Katie**, built at Duffield Bank in 1896 and withdrawn by the *Fairbourne Railway* in 1926, which will also be a great attraction to the railway when she is completed.

During the last decade two new steam locomotives were constructed for use in Japan. The first one was a 2-6-2 (akin to **Northern Rock**), as No.1 **Northern Rock II**, completed in January 1990, works plate 7/1989. The second was a similar engine, No.2 **Cumbria**, completed by December 1992, works plate 8/1992. Diesel No.3 **John Southland II** TMA 1082/1988 also ran trials in December 1988. On 17th June 1992 a small diesel 0-6-0DH locomotive had been tested on the R&ER, also for the same railway . This was No.5, **City of Birmingham**, built by TMA Engineering Ltd 5908/1992.

The Ravenglass & Eskdale Railway has been host to three overseas locomotives; two were from *Redwood Valley Railway*, California, 4-4-0 No.5 **Fern** during September 1988, and 4-6-0 No.11 **Sequoia** in 1992. Both were owned by the late Erich Thomsen. A Beyer-Garratt, Bush Mill 3, visited Ravenglass in August, 1993 from the *Bush Mill Railway*, Port Arthur in the south-east of Tasmania, a record for the longest journey ever of a miniature railway locomotive! An excellent video of the locomotive's visit was made showing the Garratt in both the U.K. and on home ground in Tasmania. Refreshments are available at both Ravenglass and Dalegarth stations.

The Ravenglass shed scene. Left, **River Esk**, *rear* **River Mite**, *right,* **Bonnie Dundee**, *(tank version),* **River Irt**, *No.1* **Northern Rock II**, *(for Shuzenji Railway of Japan), and* **Northern Rock**. *January, 1990.*

*Waiting on the centre road at Ravenglass station is **River Mite**, a smart looking 2-8-2, photographed during August, 1976.*

*Bassett-Lowke Atlantic 30 **Synolda** is carefully moved on to the turntable at Dalegarth by Peter van Zeller. This engine is part of the R&ER museum stock which still operates on special event days. As **Prince Charles** it operated for several years at the Belle Vue Railway, Manchester. 19th September, 1992.*

*The late Erich Thomsen brought his 4-4-0 No.5 **Fern** from the Redwood Valley Railway, California to operate on Britain's lengthy fifteen inch gauge railways. The support party had no idea that their locomotive would be operating in such magnificent surroundings in Cumbria, and would be running on an even longer railway in Kent. Within sight of the fells is **Fern**, having already turned on Dalegarth turntable. 15th September, 1988*

The enthusiasm shown by Erich Thomsen and the success of his previous visit to Ravenglass prompted him to bring yet another locomotive from the Redwood Valley Railway. This time Erich's No.11 4-6-0 **Sequoia** was paired with Bassett-Lowke 4-4-2 No. 30 **Synolda** on the afternoon of 19th September, 1992. Both No.5 and No.11 are oil fired machines.

Visiting RH&DR Pacific No.1 **Green Goddess** passing Muncaster Mill station, a mile from Ravenglass where this train terminated. Behind the tender is Mr. George Barlow, BEM, the driver of this fine locomotive for 31 years on the RH&DR.
3rd May, 1985.

*Motive Power Department, Ravenglass & Eskdale Railway. On the left is **River Mite** and alongside is **River Esk**. August, 1973.*

*Slowing down for a sheduled stop at The Green having brought the train from Dalegarth is **Bush Mill 3**, the visiting 0-4-0 + 0-4-0 Beyer-Garratt that was built in the Bush Mill Workshops at Port Arthur, Tasmania in 1990. The Garratt later visited the Romney, Hythe & Dymchurch Railway. The Garratt normally operates on the Bush Mill Railway which is now in a area frequented by tourists to the Island which many years ago was a penal colony.*
28th August, 1993.

Opposite page : *R.H.& D.R Pacific No.11* **Black Prince**, *made a test run on 29th April, 1982, seen here at Fisherground loop awaiting a train to cross on the main line to Dalegarth. This locomotive spent a full season at Ravenglass in 1982, exchanged with a diesel locomotive for use on the R.H.& D.R school trains.*

NORTHERN ROCK II

A milestone was established when the Ravenglass & Eskdale Railway built *Northern Rock II* for the new fifteen inch line at Niji-No-Sato, Shuzenji, in Japan. This new line was 2.4 km in length and was laid in a landscaped park as only the Japanese could do.

Above : **Northern Rock II**, now completed, seen here in the early afternoon sunlight at Ravenglass. The locomotive later worked an empty stock train to Dalegarth. 8th January 1990.

Left top : *At Ravenglass, 10th January 1990, the formal naming ceremony of **Northern Rock II**. Mr.Masaru Nagae from Japan, assisted by Mr. D.M.E Ferreira, then General Manager, Ravenglass & Eskdale Railway, carried out this happy event. (left of photograph).*

Left middle : *Dalegarth, on the footplate of No.1 **Northern Rock II** Mr.Masaru Nagae expresses his appreciation to Mrs. Mary Stalker, Mayor of Copeland. 10th January 1990.*

Left bottom: *The locomotive is seen here on 16th November, 1989 during a test run returning from Dalegarth, near Sport House bridge. A front number plate (No.1) was fitted to this engine prior to delivery. The R&ER also later built a second similar locomotive named **Cumbria** which had differently shaped works plates to No.8 dated 1992 (inset).*

*A visitor to the Ravenglass & Eskdale Railway during 1998 was the immaculate Romney, Hythe & Dymchurch Railway Pacific No.3 **Southern Maid**. Whatever the weather conditions it is always a rewarding sight to see these magnificent machines in such lovely countryside that only the fells can provide. At Muncaster, 2.5.1998.*

Rhyl Miniature Railway.   15 inch.

Marine Lake, Rhyl.

Rhyl Miniature Railway opened on May-day, 1911. Initial services were worked with a Bassett-Lowke Atlantic No.15 **Prince Edward of Wales**, and in 1913 another similar machine, No.18 **George the Fifth** arrived from the *Llewelyn Miniature Railway* at Southport. It is recorded that on 7th August, 1911 ninety-three trains were run in about eleven hours. The early history of this railway has been well covered in publications at that time, but suffice to say that larger locomotives were needed and Albert Barnes built six Atlantics at Albion Works, in Rhyl, to Greenly's design during the 1920's.

In the late 1960's there was still a formidable looking station with an overall roof and two train operation was normal practice in peak periods. Nearby was a shed that housed four locomotives, two would be in use and a third often kept in steam.

At the present time No.101 **Joan** is the only steam engine working at Rhyl, but No.103 **John** now in private ownership can occasionally be seen in steam at Ravenglass. Two others, No.102 **Railway Queen** and No.105 **Michael** are on static display in the shop at James Pringle Weavers, at Llanfair P.G. on Angelsey, No.104 **Billie** is now in private ownership in Kent, and No.106 **Billy**, was once on display inside a large glass case at the *British Rail* station at Rhyl. It is still owned by Rhyl Town Council. Over the winter period of 1998-9 **Joan** was loaned to the *Windmill Farm Railway* in Lancashire, and she returned home to Rhyl for the summer 1999 season. Happily all six Barnes have survived and five can still be seen. The railway also operates an 0-4-2T steam outline diesel locomotive built in 1961 and named **Clara**.

Extensive civil engineering work at Marine Lake was completed in 1999 after a year of closure of the railway. The track has been reinstated and now passes behind the new pumping station on a slightly different alignment.

Anti-clockwise running is a little unusual at Rhyl Miniature Railway. A viewpoint adjacent to the shed yard where **Billy** *received a moment's attention. 26th July, 1979.*

*A view of the Rhyl Miniature Railway's Marine Lake station about 1963 when two or three engines were steamed at weekends. The fare at that time was 1/6d for adults and 9d. for children. The locomotive on the right of the photograph was **Joan**.*

*A view of the present day station at Rhyl, a shadow of its former self. Here **Billy** is waiting for passengers to appear. In 1949 there were three stations at Rhyl. British Railways station in the town centre, and across the road from the RMR station was another at the Voryd Lilliput Railway, a short 11¹/₄ inch gauge line that was worked by a Caledonian 4-4-0.*

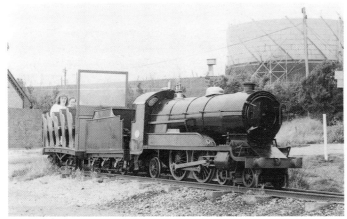

*Albert Barnes built Atlantic No. 101 **Joan** makes her way around the circuit, seen here passing the Gas Works; now demolished.*
July, 1987.

Romney, Hythe & Dymchurch Railway.

15 inch.   New Romney, Kent.

In 1927 the Romney, Hythe & Dymchurch Railway opened to traffic between Hythe and New Romney. The railway had been designed by engineer Henry Greenly for Captain J.E.P.Howey. Even in those formative years it was very difficult to construct such a line, which has been described as a main line in miniature.

The first section from Hythe to New Romney was just over 8¼ miles. The remaining 5½ miles to Dungeness was also installed as double track, which opened the following year. Captain Howey's friend Count Louis Zborowski had ordered two Pacifics from Davey Paxman of Colchester which were completed and delivered by late 1925 to New Romney, but not at the same time. During the interim period Count Zborowski died in a motoring accident and the new railway from then on became the Captain's responsibility.

In 1947 the Dungeness section (previously requisitioned by the army in 1940) was reopened with the ceremony performed by Laurel & Hardy! The up line was lifted after the war and any useful rail reinstalled on the down side, the extension becoming a single line as it is to-day. A passing loop was installed at Romney Sands in 1972.

The first two Pacifics were No. 1 **Green Goddess** and No. 2 **Northern Chief**; both were built 1925. In 1926-27 Davey Paxman built three similar locomotives, No. 3 **Southern Maid**, No. 7 **Typhoon**, and No. 8 **Hurricane**. Both **Typhoon** and **Hurricane** were originally 3 cylinder machines, the former converted to 2 cylinder operation 1935/36, and the latter in 1937. Also constructed at the same time by the same builder were a pair of 4-8-2's, No. 5 **Hercules** and No. 6 **Samson**. In 1931 Yorkshire Engine Company built two Pacifics No. 9 **Doctor Syn**, and No.10 **Black Prince**. No. 9 later became **Winston Churchill** and No. 10 was renamed **Doctor Syn**.

The name **Black Prince** was then unused until the arrival of the last Pacific, a 1937 Krupp 1664 (RH&DR No. 11), which became **Black Prince**. This locomotive was examined in

*Pacific No.8 **Hurricane** waits in Greatstone station with The Marshlander, an afternoon train from Dungeness to New Romney and Hythe. The building on the right was the UP booking office, converted to a block post by the Army c.1940. It has since been demolished, and the station closed. Photograph c.1965.*

Germany in May, 1976, and had entered traffic by September the same year. When this locomotive arrived at New Romney it still carried the nameplates *Fleissig Lieschen*, meaning Busy Lizzie! No.11 has since been rebuilt. 0-4-0 No.4 *The Bug* was originally built by Krauss in 1926.

There are in addition two large diesel locomotives, No. 12 *John Southland*, built 1983; and No. 14, (as yet unnamed), both built by TMA Engineering Ltd of Birmingham. The diesels have regular work on school trains

Nowadays, the Romney, Hythe & Dymchurch is known the world over. It has set high standards for all its locomotives and one by which all others are measured. Like most other miniature railways it has been very difficult to keep going against changing conditions; nevertheless it has survived every storm since Captain Howey's death 35 years ago. His passing was not unmarked; he left us a real main line and a beautiful set of working locomotives. Something to be really proud of.

*No.2 **Northern Chief** waits at Hythe with an afternoon train to New Romney. Note the semaphore signals.*
16th August, 1953.

*Pacific No. 9 **Winston Churchill** in the shed yard at New Romney. The fading sunlight of this late afternoon shot was still sufficient to illuminate the wheels and front end details. 2nd September, 1980.*

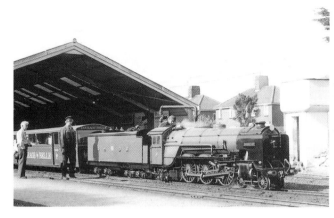

*The station clock shows 9.51am. A photographer looks on as No.8 **Hurricane** is now ready to leave New Romney for Hythe. 2nd September, 1980.*

*The spartan landscape of Dungeness has not changed much with the passage of time. This view of **Samson** was taken on 16th August, 1953.*

*In September 1977 Bassett-Lowke Little Giant **Count Louis** visited the Romney, Hythe & Dymchurch Railway during a special events weekend. This locomotive did work normal services on the Fairbourne Railway (1924-1983), it moved from there to Birmingham soon after the sale and conversion of the Fairbourne line to 12¹/₄ inch gauge.*

*Hythe is a good photographic location in the early afternoon. No.6 **Samson**, looking really immaculate, is just about ready to roll with a down train for New Romney.*
2nd September, 1980.

*The history of No.4 **The Bug** has been well documented over the past 20 years; here this little engine was turned out in green livery; looking exceedingly smart. It was photographed on the turntable at Hythe in September, 1977.*

*Another smart turnout, Pacific No.3 **Southern Maid** awaiting departure from Hythe on 12th June, 1979. This locomotive made its first visit to the Ravenglass & Eskdale Railway on 2nd May, 1998 - the last of the original batch of engines to do so.*

Saltburn Miniature Railway.   15 inch.

Saltburn-by-the-Sea, Redcar & Cleveland.

The miniature railway is situated at the lower end of the town centre at the sea front, about a ¼ mile from the main line railway station. This railway is normally operated by two diesel locomotives.

During the summer of 1997, in connection with the Victorian Celebration weekend, steam was utilised for only the second time since 1947. The invited guest was Bassett-Lowke Atlantic No.10 **Little Giant**, now repainted in maroon and owned privately, which worked several trips during a few days in August. The Saltburn line has three stations, Cat Nab, Bridge Halt and Valley Gardens, all quite close to each other; a passing loop allows two train running alongside the stock sheds. Run round loops are used at each terminal point. The railway is quite open along most of its route - about ½ mile in length.

Very much a hi-day at Saltburn when Bassett-Lowke class 10 Atlantic Little Giant brought steam to this short railway. It was a Victorian weekend and even at the main line station an LMS 8F 2-8-0 No. 48151 was on display!

Steamtown Miniature Railway.   15 inch.

Carnforth, Lancashire.   (At the former BR mpd).

*Bassett-Lowke 4-4-2 No. 22 **Princess Elizabeth**, then recently ex-shops, poses for the camera at a point beyond Carnforth shed yard.*

The first section of this railway opened in 1977. It is about a mile in length and was still being extended during a very inclement day on 25th, February, 1979, when Bassett-Lowke No. 18 *George the Fifth* was in steam working an engineers' train.

The railway operates from Northgate station, at the entrance to Steamtown Carnforth, adjacent to a miniature signal box named Carnforth Box No.1 where there is a platform and run round loop. From here, the line veers away from the entrance gate, along the western side of the shed yard. At this point the line passes through the standard gauge shed, southbound to another station, Steamtown, with a passing loop alongside the SMR workshops. Here there is a traverser for movement of engines into the shed.

The line continues along the periphery of the site towards Green Ayre Halt and onwards to Crag Bank where there is a run round loop situated alongside the standard gauge station. Cosmetic signals exist at some of the stations. The miniature platform is at a lower level than the standard gauge demonstration line, here passengers could change trains, Crag Bank was an interchange, itself unusual on a miniature railway.

Three steam locomotives were used. One of them, which had been at Carnforth since 1982, was Guest Engineering Pacific No.9/1949, 4-6-2 *Prince William* . In August 1982 smoke deflectors were fitted but these were subsequently removed. In July 1983 the engine was painted green; in later years it became maroon with large cab side numerals. The next move was to Bury during August 1995 prior to the closure of Carnforth shed to the public in 1997, and it is now a regular working engine at the *Windmill Farm Railway*.

A Bassett-Lowke Class 20 Atlantic No.22 *Princess Elizabeth* has worked the line on occasions, a duty shared with Bassett-Lowke No. 18 *George the Fifth.* The railway also has two diesel locomotives. At the time of writing the future of this railway is rather uncertain. A $7^{1}/_{4}$ inch gauge railway was installed in a field beyond the SMR near the halt. This railway, operated by a local model engineering society from about 1982-1996, has been removed. The latter has been relocated north of Carnforth near the A6.

When Bassett-Lowke No. 18 **George the Fifth** *was restored it was painted blue and lettered M.R.G.B. (Miniature Railways of Great Britain). It has been at Carnforth for some years now, seen here with a good head of steam in the winter sunlight. 25th February, 1979*

An engine that seems to have been everywhere. Guest Pacific 5751, without name plates, makes its way past the open fields towards Crag Bank Low Level station. The engine would then run round to return tender first towards Carnforth shed yard.

Waveney Valley Railway.   15 inch.

Bressingham Gardens, Diss, Norfolk.

The longest journey by miniature railway at Bressingham is the two mile clockwise circuit of their 15 inch system which operates through the estate, crossing at one point the 2ft. narrow gauge line. The return journey towards the terminal station passes alongside the standard gauge demonstration line where it is sometimes possible to see main line locomotives at work.

The locomotives for the Waveney Valley Railway are two Krupp 4-6-2's built in 1937, No.1662 named ***Rösenkavalier***, and No.1663 ***Mannertreu***. Both were from Gruga Park, Essen, and were purchased in Germany with 19 coaches in 1972. They are impressive machines and carry a dark green livery with black and white lining. Now on display inside the museum is LNER A3 Pacific 4472 ***Flying Scotsman***, built to ¼ scale by Washington Metal Works in 1976. A 10¼ inch gauge railway has also been established at Bressingham.

*The Waveney Valley Railway is normally operated by one of the two Krupp Pacifics. This photograph, a quarter of a century ago, shows 1663 **Mannertreu** at work within the grounds.*
26th August, 1973.
Courtesy : A.Bloom

Whorlton Lido. 15 inch.

Near Barnard Castle, Co.Durham.

Bassett-Lowke 4-4-2 Class 20 **King George** originally came from Southport and during August, 1976 was kept in immaculate condition, with original paint work and tender lettering Lakeside Miniature Railway. It was normally the working steam locomotive on this $^1/_2$ mile railway.

Trains start and terminate at Whorlton Halt, from where the railway follows a winding circuit, passing through a tunnel before taking the through road at Whorlton Halt and onwards past the locomotive department, where a trailing connection leaves the main line. The railway is situated in a very pleasant location close to the rocky banks of the Tees.

The late Mr.Raymond Dunn, a keen miniature steam man acquired another Atlantic No.103 **John** (in green livery) which came from Alton Towers. This was one of the six Barnes locomotives built at Rhyl in the 1920's and used at the Rhyl Miniature Railway, reaching Whorlton Lido March 1985. **John** is sometimes a visitor at the Ravenglass & Eskdale Railway. In 1976 Mr.W.Stewart's Pacific No.4472 LNER **Flying Scotsman**, built Washington Metal Works 1976, a $^1/_4$ scale locomotive, ran initial trials on the railway prior to joining the Grand Cavalcade on 25th September of that year on the Ravenglass & Eskdale Railway. No. 4472 left Whorlton Lido in 1979. The railway is still in operation with a diesel locomotive.

King George, one of the two surviving Bassett-Lowke Class 20 Atlantics from Southport. It was well cared for at Whorlton Lido, and still lettered Lakeside Miniature Railway. Photographed on a very warm afternoon in July, 1976.

LNER A3 Pacific 4472 **Flying Scotsman**, a very attractive engine of $^1/_4$ scale, worked some of the trains at Whorlton Lido whilst running in. August, 1976.

On the through road, A3 Pacific 4472 **Flying Scotsman** at speed passing Whorlton Halt with a full complement of passengers. August, 1976.

Barnes Atlantic No. 103 **John** came to Whorlton Lido from Alton Towers, still in green livery. On this occasion it was an uphill push from the shed into the afternoon sunlight for photography! 13th September, 1986.

Windmill Farm Railway.   15 inch.
Red Cat Lane, Burscough, West Lancashire.
(The 15 inch Gauge Heritage Centre)

Initial construction of a new fifteen inch railway commenced in June, 1996; the work being carried out by Mr. A. Moss. The work was programmed over three phases; the first two were completed by the end of 1997. The main station is at Windmill Farm, here there is a passing loop with a turn out to the maintenance section and carriage sheds. The booking office is located at the end of the station.

From this point the railway becomes a single line swinging away across the meadows towards the Windmill, once steam driven and without sails. Onwards the line passes through a gateway towards the next station, Lakeview, which has a passing loop. Here an extensive lake has been created, the railway when completed will follow the periphery of the lake to rejoin the main line again. Some of the rail used was recovered from the now closed *Dudley Zoo Railway.*

The first steam locomotive to run on the railway was Barnes Atlantic No. 101 *Joan* from Rhyl which worked light engine over the line on 7th September, 1997 and again on the 14th when she was used on a works construction train during the afternoon. The first double header operated was a Christmas Special to *Lakeview* on 21st December hauled by 2-8-0PH *St. Nicholas* (SL 15/5/78) and 4-6-2DE *Duke of Edinburgh* (H.N.Barlow of 1950). A former Liverpool International Garden Festival coach fully restored was used to convey invited guests on this historic occasion. A second similar vehicle has since entered service.

By 23rd May, 1998, Guest Pacific No. 5751 **Prince William** had joined the fleet becoming the railway's first active steam locomotive. Visiting locomotives on this date included Barnes Atlantic *Joan* and Bassett-Lowke 4-4-2 No. 30 **Synolda** from the *Ravenglass & Eskdale*

The first steam engine to work at Windmill Farm Railway was Barnes Atlantic No. 101 **Joan***, seen here working an engineers' train. The van (ex. Fairbourne Railway) was from the Haigh Hall Railway at Wigan, Lancashire. 14th September, 1997.*

Railway. Another H.N.Barlow locomotive of 1962 named **Princess Anne** is now restored and provided the opportunity of double heading with **Duke of Edinburgh**.

During the summer of 1998 a Bay platform was commissioned, the run round loop extended and two open coaches ex-*Dudley Zoo Railway* have been fully restored. Four former 12¼ inch Fairbourne passenger coaches have been added to the existing fleet and modified to the larger gauge. A turntable was installed during October, 1998, this now allows access to a covered area where facilities will be provided for a display and exhibition of rolling stock.

In March, 1999 a Cagney 4-4-0 built c.1902 No.44 of the *Lancaster & Chester Railroad*, Springs Park, Fort Mill, South Carolina arrived in the UK. This locomotive was purchased at an American public auction for eventual use on the Windmill Farm Railway. The Cagney when restored will be a great attraction to the railway. A number of these useful small engines are known to have operated in America from the turn of the century, but in Britain they were quite rare. Two open coaches to run with No.44 were obtained from the *Bredgar & Wormshill Railway* in Kent.

A Battery-Electric Class 5 LMS 4-6-0 No. 5305 was built by Mr. Austin Moss during 1998/99 for a 15 inch gauge private railway in Vancouver, Canada. This locomotive operates with a 24 Volt electrical system and a chain drive, the battery storage area being inside the boiler cladding. The motion and some other parts have been chrome plated at the request of the purchaser. It is likely that No. 5305 is the first electrically powered Class 5. It was on view at the Windmill Farm Railway Gala weekend 12/13th June, 1999.

It is an interesting railway with a lot to offer. Light refreshments are available when the farm is open. A site entry fee applies.

*Pacific 5751 **Prince William** heads an afternoon train from Windmill Farm towards Lakeview on 13th September, 1998. The Farm is now a popular location where there are various attractive animals, many being seen from the railway. The Windmill, off the picture to the left; can be seen from North Western Trains on the former L&YR line between New Lane and Bescar Lane stations.*

In the open countryside heading towards the Windmill is 4-6-2 **Princess Anne**, built by Barlow, photographed looking east on 13th September, 1998. Until the railway is completed the locomotives have to return from Lakeview tender first.

Steam outline 2-8-0PH **St. Nicholas** returning to Windmill Farm station hauling a recently restored former Liverpool Garden Festival coach. 14th September, 1997.

On the run round loop is 1962 Barlow Pacific **Princess Anne**, awaiting the return train from Lakeview to Windmill Farm station. Since this photograph was taken engines can now stand clear of the main line on the recently completed Bay platform track. 13th September, 1998.

On 23rd May, 1998 steam double-heading became possible at the Windmill Farm Railway;
*Atlantic Joan, then recently lettered R.M.R was piloting 4-4-2 **Synolda** on a return working*
from Lakeview.

*A new LMS Class 5 4-6-0, battery powered, **No.5305** was placed on the recently constructed*
turntable at Windmill Farm Railway, in connection with the Gala event of 12/13th June 1999.
It is expected that 5305 will leave the railway before the millennium, becoming the first 15 inch
gauge Class 5 to cross the Atlantic, where it will have a new home in Canada.

Sutton Miniature Railway.   15 inch.

(Locomotives illustrated at other than their original railway)

Of particular interest it is worth mentioning the two Atlantics surviving from the Sutton Miniature Railway, closed in 1962. No.1 **Sutton Belle** and No.2 **Sutton Flyer** have been stored unseen (with one known exception) for the past 36 years. **Sutton Belle** made a surprise visit at Tyseley on 7th October, 1973 during a special events weekend when standard gauge LNER A3 4472 **Flying Scotsman** was on display alongside *Romney, Hythe & Dymchurch Railway* fifteen inch gauge Pacific No.3 **Southern Maid**.

It is a quarter of a century since Atlantic No.1 Sutton Belle was displayed at Tyseley in late 1973. On arrival, ropes had been placed around the locomotive which by agreement with the lorry driver were carefully removed for a few minutes whilst this photograph was taken.

Sutton Miniature Railway No.2 Sutton Flyer arrived at New Romney on 1st June, 1959 and worked on the RH&DR until 4th June; leaving on the 5th. On 3rd June, 1959 Sutton Flyer had worked a round trip of the railway, the driver was Jim Glover; seen here talking to Bill Hunt outside New Romney signal box. The engine was waiting to be turned in order to work another journey to Hythe and back. The coach was a Heywood vehicle, at the time based at New Romney.

Courtesy: George A. Barlow, BEM.

LITTLE TITAN

*The 15inch gauge steam Crane named **Little Titan** was completed by E.Cheeseman of Peterlee, County Durham by 1975 and was displayed that year at the Stockton & Darlington 150 Exhibition. In connection with the Ravenglass & Eskdale Railway Centenary of 1976 the Crane was steamed within the station limits at Ravenglass. The present location of this very useful machinery is the Bure Valley Railway in Norfolk, where eventually it could operate with the R.O.D 2-8-0 Class 04 when completed in due course.*

Chapter 2
12¹/₄, 12 and 11¹/₄ inch Gauges

12¹/₄ inch

Exmoor Steam Railway

Fairbourne & Barmouth Railway

Littlehampton Miniature Railway

Nickelodeon Line, Ashorne Hall

12 inch

Barkby Garden Rail Road

Olicana Railway

11¹/₄ inch

Voryd Lilliput Railway

Exmoor Steam Railway. $12^{1}/_{4}$ inch.

Bratton Fleming, North Devon.

The main station is Exmoor Town, it is undercover and adjacent to a comfortable seating area where there are buffet and gift shop facilities. The railway, opened in August, 1990 is partly on an embankment following a course around a double looped section which is steeply graded in places. Good use has been made of the site which provided an inspiring one mile journey with enclosed stock.

Nearby is the workshop accommodation where several new $7^{1}/_{4}$, $10^{1}/_{4}$, $12^{1}/_{4}$ and 15 inch gauge engines, including passenger rolling stock, have been constructed for other railways. Resident locomotives at the end of the 1993 season were 2-8-0T No. 190 **Yeo Valley** and an 0-6-0T No. 191, **Lorna Doone**, of 1991. A new station, Cape of Good Hope, has since opened on this site.

*Steam on Exmoor! No.191 **Lorna Doone** takes the grade in her stride; a scenic location a short distance from Exmoor Town station. 16th September, 1993.*

EXMOOR STEAM RAILWAY.
EXMOOR TOWN (return) 8
The holder is entitled to unlimited
Train rides on day of issue. This 9
ticket is not transferable. All children
under 8 must be accompanied by an adult 9
at all times. Dogs must be kept on a lead.
BRATTON FLEMING, N. DEVON
Tel. Brayford (0598) 710711 1
Thank you for visiting our railway. 1

Fairbourne & Barmouth Railway.

Fairbourne, Merionethshire.   12¼ inch.

(Previously 15 inch gauge)

Mr. John Ellerton purchased the Fairbourne Railway in January 1984; the new company operated the 15 inch gauge system for the next year using existing motive power and stock. **Count Louis** and **Ernest W.Twining** were not purchased by the new company and both these engines were stored, the former for a period remained at Fairbourne and the latter was sold to a new railway in Japan. This left 2-4-2s **Katie** and **Siân** as working steam locomotives.

As a short-term attraction **Siân** was rebuilt as an American outline locomotive becoming No.362, **Sydney**. The tender was lettered *Sea Train*, livery black and silver and a water bag hung outside the cab side sheet. The conversion was carried out at Fairbourne. In 1985 **Sydney** was disposed of to Littlecote House, at Hungerford. In 1984 **Katie** was re-named **Shôn,** and afterwards sold (as previously mentioned) to the *Haigh Hall Railway* at Wigan, Lancashire, in 1985, where she was re-named **Haigh Hall**.

By 1986 the former *Fairbourne Railway* had been re-gauged to 12¼ inch. New buildings were erected at Fairbourne and other changes were made. The steam stock assembled at Fairbourne had been built for the new owner's previous railway - the *Réseau Guerlédan Chemin de Fer Touristque*, in Brittany.

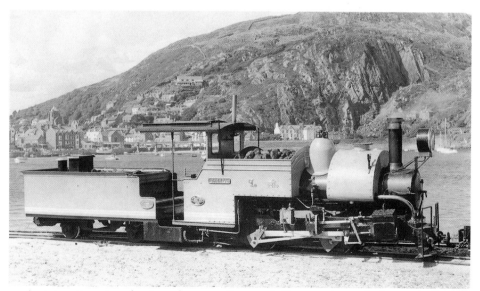

*An interesting view showing **Sherpa** at Barmouth Ferry, against a background of the Mawddach estuary and the town of Barmouth. In this view the locomotive was complete with builder's plate, Milner Engineering Chester Ltd, No. 106/1978. Photographed 5th August, 1987.*

These were 0-4-0ST *France* built by Milner Engineering Chester Ltd. as No. 106 of 1978 and renamed *Sherpa* by 1985. 2-6-2T *Jubilee*, built by David Curwen, No. 1078 of 1978, which at Fairbourne became Southern No. 759 *Yeo.* 0-6-4ST *David Curwen*, later renamed *Beddgelert*; built by David Curwen; 1279 of No. 1979, and No.5, a Leek & Manifold 2-6-4T named *Elaine*. The latter was delivered to Fairbourne in 1984 and stored alongside *David Curwen* at the station on a short section of 12¼ inch gauge track. *Elaine* was a nice looking engine with a superb finish built by Milner Engineering Chester Ltd as No. 108 of 1979. Regretfully she did not run in that form and was rebuilt as the present *Russell*.

One new locomotive was built at Fairbourne - No.24, a 2-6-2 Sandy River built in 1990, originally to 12¼ inch gauge. This locomotive was sold from Fairbourne and has been re-gauged to 15 inch having worked on the *Bure Valley Railway*, later at *Kirklees Light Railway* (as No.2). She now has a new permanent home at the *Cleethorpes Coast Light Railway,* and now restored to her former black livery, regaining the original number 24. A new owner, Dr. Roger Melton obtained the Fairbourne & Barmouth Railway in 1995.

2-6-2T Yeo as Southern Railway No.759, viewed here against the background of Barmouth Bridge carrying the former British Railways line from Machynlleth to Barmouth and Pwllheli. 5th August, 1987.

*2-6-4T No.5 **Russell** was photographed alongside the passing loop, the shadow on the left is from the sea wall; a pleasant vantage point on a cloudless day.*
9th September, 1988.

*0-6-4T No.2 **Beddgelert** is on the return journey from Barmouth Ferry proceeding towards the passing loop and onwards to Fairbourne. At this point the public road is on the right which leads to a convenient car park at the end.*
5th August, 1987.

Littlehampton Miniature Railway. 12¹/₄ inch.

Mewsbrook Park, Littlehampton, West Sussex.

This long established seaside line was opened in 1948. In early 1969 the railway was offered for sale by Mead & Turner Ltd., the owner at that time. It has a 900 yard track with two stations, one at Norfolk Road and the other at Mewsbrook Park. From the main station the railway follows a course towards Sea Road terminating opposite the Pavilion in sight of the beach. The steam locomotives were a pair of 4-6-4s built by John Thurston to 12¹/₄ inch gauge, No. 1005 *Gordon* and No. 2010 *Henry*. Both had eight wheel tenders; the engines were similar to each other and *Gordon* had smoke deflectors. No. 1005 was in blue livery and 2010 green.

On Sunday, 12th September, 1976 Flooks 4-4-2 *Prince Edward* was outside the running shed, ex-*Olicana Railway*, Ilkley still in the same livery, along with two 7¹/₄ inch locomotives, a 4-4-4 No.1955 *Grimsby Town* and 4-6-4 No.1947 *Henrietta*. Both the 7¹/₄ inch locomotives were built by J.Newbutt. The reason for these engines being outside in very clean condition became apparent on finding they had been specially placed earlier that day for an official photographer preparing illustrations for a new brochure! No.1955 later moved to Cheals Garden & Leisure Centre, Pulborough and 1947 went into private ownership in the Lake District. *Prince Edward* moved on to South Coast World and later to a private owner in the South of England. The railway is still in use with a petrol locomotive.

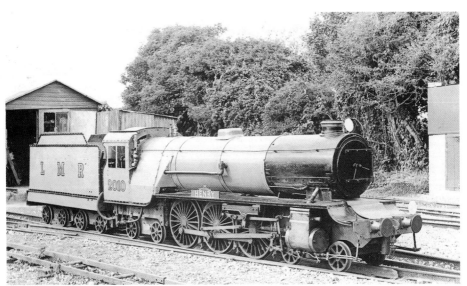

*A photographer's dream! 2010 **Henry** in a "rods down" situation in bright sunlight on 12th September, 1976.*

Flookes Atlantic **Prince Edward** *was rediscovered at Littlehampton Miniature Railway although of 12 inch gauge. Three years earlier this locomotive had seen service at Ilkley on the Olicana Railway. 12th September, 1976.*

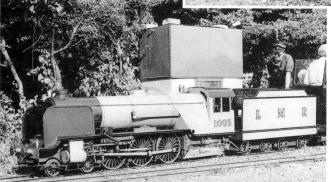

On 12th September, 1976 No.1005 **Gordon** *was the locomotive in steam at Littlehampton Miniature Railway.*

On the 12th September 1976 there were two 7¹/₄ inch gauge locomotives at the 12¹/₄ inch gauge Littlehampton Miniature Railway! One was No. 1955, a 4-4-4 named **Grimsby Town**.

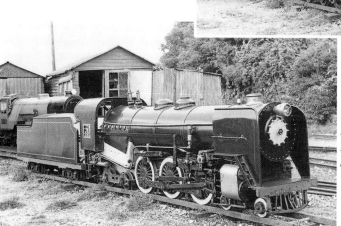

The other 7¹/₄ inch gauge locomotive was a 4-6-4 No.1947 **Henrietta** *in very clean condition.*

Nickelodeon Line, Ashorne Hall Railway.

12¹/₄ inch.   near Warwick.

This is an interesting railway where good use has been made of available land. The railway is about ³/₄ mile in length with two stations, Orange Blossom Halt and New Lodge. There is one steam locomotive, a 2-4-2T named **Ashorne** built by Exmoor Steam Railway, No. 297/94 in maroon livery, and a petrol locomotive.

The coaching stock was built locally to a very high standard. The coaches are unusual with ornate open ends finished in green/teak with drop down side windows, contrasting with their grey roofs. The journey is quite scenic; the line passing over a bridge and beyond into parkland where photographic possibilities are good. The Hall caters for those particularly interested in musical works with a Nickelodeon Collection. It has very good catering facilities.

*It is a delightful journey around the woodlands of Ashorne Hall in Springtime. This scene showing the resident steam locomotive 2-4-2T **Ashorne** illustrates how the railway has been fitted into its surroundings. The locomotive runs alternate trips bunker first. Well worthy of a visit. 7th May, 1995.*

Barkby Garden Rail Road.   12 inch. (nominal)

Malt Shovel Hotel, Barkby, Leicestershire.

A short railway existed at the rear of the Malt Shovel Hotel within the garden area during August, 1976. It was a single line about 60 yards in length running from the Hotel where the locomotive was housed in an out building. The railway was on a gradual right hand curve terminating within the limit of the garden. The locomotive was numbered 69665 named **Little Eva**, a 4-4-0 very likely built by R.H.Morse. It was a heavy engine and difficult to push into the open. Her livery was black with red, very little is known about her and she appears to have been sold sometime in 1977 to a buyer in Belgium. Present whereabouts not known.

*Barkby Garden Rail Road. In the garden of the Malt Shovel, 4-4-0 No. 69665 **Little Eva** was used occasionally during summer evenings. The line was very short with limited photographic opportunities.15th August, 1976.*

Olicana Railway.   12 inch.

Ilkley, West Yorkshire.

There was one steam locomotive on this 'L' shaped railway, a Flooks 4-4-2 named ***Prince Edward*** which operated following the periphery of a field close to the River Wharfe. The Atlantic was in use on 7th August, 1973. Only one passenger coach was used, the train working a pull/push service. ***Prince Edward*** moved to the *Littlehampton Miniature Railway* and afterwards to *South Coast World* at Bognor Regis (new name for Butlins Camp). The railway has since closed. The locomotive is now in private ownership.

*Action at Ilkley! Flookes Atlantic **Prince Edward** gathers momentum close to the River Wharfe 25 years ago.*

The Voryd Lilliput Railway.   11¼ inch.

Amusement Park, Rhyl.

Described at the time as the Smallest Train In Daily Service. The railway had only one locomotive, a Caledonian 4-4-0 **No. 769**, likely built by D. Croall about 1900, which operated on about 60 yards of track within the amusement park complex, facing towards the sea. It was an out and back journey with one station, and was in use during 1948-1950. However, the locomotive very soon vanished from the scene, seemingly into oblivion, but it did survive after closure of the line.

No. 769 spent a number of years in a private garage in Cheshire before being fully restored to steam at Springvale Mill in Haslingden, Lancashire, during August, 1988. There it was repainted in blue *Caledonian Railway* livery. A hundred years on since building and this unusual 4-4-0 can still be found on display inside a glass case at the Museum of Transport, Glasgow.

It is almost half a century ago since this historic photograph was taken on 2nd August, 1949 of Caledonian Railway 4-4-0 No. 769 on the Voryd Lilliput Railway at Rhyl. It is true to say that very few illustrations exist of this unique line with a most unusual gauge of 11¼ inches.
Courtesy : Neville Fields

It is likely that C.R. 4-4-0 No. 769 left Rhyl sometime in 1950. Thirty eight years later final restoration work was completed. 18th August, 1988.

Chapter 3

10$^1/_4$ inch Gauge

Age of Steam

Audley End Miniature Railway

Bickington Steam Railway

Blackberry Line, Chichester

Carlyon Bay Min)ature Railway

Dinting Railway Centre

Ferry Meadows Railway

Hastings Miniature Railway

Kerrs Miniature Railway

Leek & Manifold Railway

Littlestone Miniature Railway

Lower Peover Fete

Mull & West Highland N. G. Railway

The Narrower Gauge Railway

Newby Hall Miniature Railway

North Midland Railway

Oakhill Manor Railway

Orchard Farm Railway

Royal Victoria Railway

Rudyard Lake Miniature Railway

Rudyard Lake Railway(2nd)

Shibdon Hall Miniature Railway

Southend Miniature Railway

Stapleford Park Miniature Railway

Suffolk Wildlife Park

Syon Park Miniature Railway

Thoresby Hall Railway

Towans Railway

Watford Miniature Railway

Wells Harbour Railway

Wells & Walsingham Railway

Age of Steam.   10¹/₄ inch.

Crowlas, Near Penzance.
formally Crowlas Woodland Railway.

Opened May, 1977. Some of the rolling stock came from the *Shillingstone Light Railway* in 1975. Steam motive power used on this line was 0-6-2T **Kingsley**, built by Minimum Gauge Railways, No.80 of 1975; this unusually large engine had been tested on the *Stapleford Miniature Railway* when new and seen there on 15th August, 1976. At Age of Steam it became No.3 **Trevithick**, moving eventually to *Watford Miniature Railway* and later sold. No.4 was a 1977 built Curwen 2-6-0, painted green with yellow lining named **Isambard Kingdom Brunel**. The tender was lettered CWR (Crowlas Woodland Railway) and the locomotive was working the line on 22nd August, 1979.

Three passenger coaches were in use on this occasion painted brown and cream fulfilling the mock GWR image. There was one station. The railway formed a circuit of about a mile around the site. Both the steam locomotives were housed in a shed adjacent to the station. The railway had a relatively short life and was eventually closed in 1984. **Isambard Kingdom Brunel** is now back in service and can be seen working at the *Royal Victoria Railway*, Netley, Hants.

*No.4 **Isambard Kingdom Brunel** returns with a full passenger load after a journey around the circuit. This locomotive has now reached its new home at the Royal Victoria Railway.*

Audley End Miniature Railway.   10¹/₄ inch.

Near Saffron Walden, Essex.

Photographs by special arrangement with Lord Braybrooke

Lord Braybrooke often drives on the Audley End Railway. This illustration shows a train from Audley End station approaching Whitehouse Curve. 20th April, 1992.

The Audley End Railway was constructed during 1963 and opened to traffic on 16th May the following year. The inaugural train was worked by Curwen Atlantic No. 3548 **Gordon**, driven by the well known racing driver Stirling Moss, OBE. The Atlantic was one of a batch of seven built in the early post war years, having earlier seen service at Southend. This locomotive was rebuilt during 1981 to a 2-6-2 and renamed **Lord Braybrooke.**

The original layout was extended in 1979 to its present length of 1¹/₂ miles, running through extensive woodlands after crossing the Rivers Fulfen and Cam.

Deep in the parkland there is a low level single platform at Forest Deep Halt, a delightful little miniature railway station complete with its small passengers who watch all the trains go by. For all the young children there are faces galore around the line and in the trees. At Audley End station, there is an extensive track layout complete with a miniature signal box, and scale signals. From this point visitors can view the arrival of incoming trains in a superb setting. Here, all passengers commence their journey. Lord Braybrooke is a regular driver along with dedicated staff who assist in lighting up the engines and preparing them for the day ahead.

There is an interesting motive power depot situated a short distance from the main station, with a most exciting selection of locomotives, including a Great Northern Atlantic as LNER No. 4433 and L.N.W.R (George the Fifth) No. 1680 **Loyalty**, both built by David Curwen, the latter in 1994. Weekend trains are usually hauled by 2-6-2 No 24 **Linda** , Rio Grande 2-8-2 No. 489 **Sara Lucy** or **Lord Braybrooke.** A new 2-4-2 was built during 1996/7 named **Barbara Curwen** after David Curwen's wife.

Retired from active service is the only $10^1/_4$ inch gauge Great Western Star No. 4005 **Polar Star**, a genuine 4 cylinder engine, built in 1989 by David Curwen - a gem in the galaxy of miniature railways.

A $7^1/_4$ inch miniature railway operates occasionally at weekends on a site adjacent to Audley End Miniature Railway station; a Great Eastern J.15 0-6-0 has operated here.

Denver & Rio Grande Western Railway No.489 **Sara Lucy** *is a powerful locomotive demonstrating her ability to haul quite heavy trains on the Audley End Railway, a requirement on busy Sunday afternoons in the season. 3rd April, 1983.*

Forest Deep Halt is the only wayside station on the railway. It has its own booking office and there are always a few passengers waiting! 20th April, 1992.

In springtime the Audley End woodlands are superb when the daffodils are in bloom. Now a 2-6-2 and a much improved engine, rebuilt Curwen No. 3548 **Lord Braybrooke** is seen in action.

*LNWR No. 1680 **Loyalty** and the GN Atlantic pause for a brief photographic stop on the final curve before entering Audley End station. It is very seldom that double heading of trains on this railway occurs. This was a special event arranged by Lord Braybrooke on 8th July, 1996.*

*An immaculate Great Western - the only known 10¼ inch gauge Star 4-6-0 No. 4005 **Polar Star** was built by David Curwen and used albeit briefly on the Audley End Railway. This photograph shows the locomotive outside the running shed on 17th August, 1991. This very much scale machine has since been placed on display elsewhere on the Estate.*

Bickington Steam Railway.   10^1/$_4$ inch.

Trago Mills, Newton Abbot, Devon.

The Bickington Steam Railway is a major attraction within the Trago Mills site. It has a well constructed station similar to Great Western style with two platforms, a footbridge and a computerised signalling system. Trains run as required; the railway which opened in 1988 has been extended in recent years giving a route length of over a mile. Some of the stock came from *Rudyard Lake Railway* via Kessingland.

The Coleby Simkins Engineering ex-Rudyard Lake 2-6-4T No.1 ***E.R.Calthrop*** of 1974 and 1948 built Curwen Atlantic No. 750 ***Blanche of Lancaster*** both came from Kessingland, along with a 1984 Simkins & Vere 2-6-0 ***Alice***. A Sandy River 2-6-2 **No.24** came additionally to the railway in 1991, also a diesel locomotive is in use. On the site are extensive workshop facilities, and a turntable. An extra attraction is model land where a 7^1/$_4$ inch gauge LMS Class 5 4-6-0 No.5157 ***The Glasgow Highlander*** is on display inside a glass case. An entry charge is made to visit this large, well constructed, illuminated model railway.

*Bickington Railway station Platform 1, 2-6-0 **Alice** is ready to depart with a rake of closed stock. The station has been built to a high standard, it is controlled by colour light signals and has a GWR appearance.*
7th September, 1989.

*The Bickington Steam Railway has a few secluded vantage points where it is possible to photograph the railway.   This rather attractive spot is quite close to the station where the line crosses a large water display; beneath are various species of fish and above **Alice** makes her way around the extensive circuit.*

The Blackberry Line.   10¹/₄ & 7¹/₄ inch.

The Hornet, Chichester, West Sussex.

(Operated by Chichester & District Society of Model Engineers Ltd.)

A dual gauge 830ft railway forms an oval around the periphery of this site. There is one station named Chichester which has a passing loop; here all passengers board the train. A journey comprises two circuits of the railway. This railway though is unique having as motive power a 10¹/₄ inch gauge 4-4-0 built in 1908 by Mr.R.A.Briggs, AMI Mech. E and his son Mr.R.W.Briggs. The locomotive, No.1 *Winnie* was named after one of Mr. Briggs' daughters.

Winnie was operated for a season during 1909 by Mr. Briggs' son at Bognor, the first miniature railway at that resort. It was known as the *Bognor Model Railway*. The locomotive has cylinders from a steam car and a similar spare unit was on display during the Golden Jubilee celebrations of the Chichester and District Society of Model Engineers in August, 1998. The locomotive's original boiler and the one that followed were built to Mr.Briggs' own design; similar "Briggs" boilers are used in miniature locomotives to-day.

Winnie, now 91 years old and one of the oldest working engines, is cared for by dedicated members of the society. She is not very well known by miniature railway enthusiasts, having been used from 1913 until 1956 on Mr.R.A.Briggs' private *Shripney Railway*, about 2 miles north of Bognor Regis. During 1963 the locomotive came to Chichester, and by 1978 the 10¹/₄ inch track of the Blackberry Line became operational and *Winnie* was provided with a new home.

A Warship class Bo-Bo diesel, No.863

Here, 4-4-0 Winnie pauses at Chichester station in the late morning sunlight, on 15th August, 1998.

Warrior, works the 7¹/₄ inch gauge line and there are facilities for the operationof 3¹/₂ and 5 inch gauge locomotives on raised track. The railway is open to the public during the operating season on the last Sunday of the month, a nominal entry fee applies.

A recommended visit!

Chichester Model Engineers' Golden Jubilee celebrations. One of the highlights at this event was the steaming of their 1908 built 4-4-0 No.1 **Winnie**, *a locomotive constructed over a three year period by Mr.Robert Alexander Briggs, AMI Mech. E and his son, Mr.Robert Westrope Briggs. This locomotive is unique in having the cylinders from a steam car. At a healthy 91 years old,* **Winnie** *is a great attraction. Photographed with driver Alan Edwards on 15th August, 1998.*

Dinting Railway Centre.   10¹/₄ inch.

Dinting, near Glossop, Derbyshire. (Temporary Installation).

The only miniature railway at Dinting was a weekend event in June, 1972 when Jack Doyle of Manchester brought Curwen Atlantic No. 2005 to operate over a short length of portable track situated where eventually No.4 road, the Centre's standard gauge running line was under construction. A new 3-car articulated set with fibreglass seats was obtained in 1972 from Coleby Simkins, and used that year at three other locations, at Burtonwood, Chelford and Poynton Park; the latter in connection with a campaign to keep Poynton in Cheshire.

The 4-4-2 along with Curwen Pacific No. 2001 **Robin Hood** left Weymouth during 1971 to be stored over the winter in Manchester. No. 2005 was sold to the *North Midland Railway* at Loughborough; operating over a short 10¹/₄ inch gauge railway within the confines of the Great Central station using the same stock.

By July, 1973 the Atlantic became No.196 **Waverley**. The new owner carried out further restoration work which included repainting to brown livery. A later move found **Waverley** at the *Mull & West Highland Narrow Gauge Railway,* Craignure on the Isle of Mull off the west coast of Scotland. An elevated model railway operated for some years on a site within Dinting Railway Centre. The Centre is now closed.

Jack Doyle's Curwen Atlantic No. 2005 seen here at Dinting operating on portable track.

Carlyon Bay Miniature Railway.   10¹/₄ inch.

Near St.Austell, Cornwall.

One of the two *Dudley Zoo Railway* Atlantics, No. 1002 had reached Carlyon Bay around 1959. There was a running shed situated on slightly higher ground for the 4-4-2 and a diesel. The railway was in the sandy environment of the beach; it had been extended to allow about a ¹/₄ mile run. At Carlyon Bay the locomotive carried the No. 289; it was still operational in late 1979 and appeared to deputise for the diesel as necessary. No.289 carried a maroon livery looking quite smart, the railway however became a victim of storm damage and did not operate during the 1992 season. The railway has since closed, the exact date uncertain, and the whereabouts of No. 289 are unknown.

The tranquil scene of almost twenty years ago on the seashore at Carlyon Bay. Atlantic No. 289 was in use on the railway on 21st August, 1979.

Ferry Meadows Railway.   10¹/₄ inch.

Nene Park, Peterborough, Cambridgeshire.

This railway provides a useful service for visitors, as well as an attraction in its own right, and was opened in May, 1979. It is approximately ¹/₂ mile in length, commencing at Ham Lane station, built on a curve with a run round loop. Adjacent to the station is the stock shed and turntable.

Leaving Ham Lane the line passes a play area for children, then swings northwards towards Lynch Lake where Lynch station once existed, long since removed at an undetermined date. The end of the journey is at Gunwade Lake station, where there are run round facilities and at the very end a turntable. Quite heavy trains operate over the railway which has a ruling gradient of 1 in 70 down from Ham Lane. The railway is quite open for most of its length; photographic possibilities are good.

The first locomotive was built by E. Dove in 1950 as a 4-6-4 named **Commodore Vanderbilt.** It was rebuilt in 1981 as a 4-6-2 and fitted with smoke deflectors; on the smokebox a small headboard indicated *Lakes Express.* It has since become No. 1950 and re-named **Henry**. A second engine, an 'Alice' class Hunslet 0-4-0ST **Ivor** was built over a period of fifteen years by Denis Jones and Alex Mills. This locomotive was operational in the early 1990's and had joined the railway by 1997. A diesel locomotive was sold during the Spring of 1999, and a new diesel locomotive has since been ordered.

A *Darjeeling Himalayan Railway* 'B' class 0-4-0ST No.797 is under construction by Laurence Hall to be named **Darjeeling**; it will carry a livery of blue with double white stripes. This locomotive is expected to operate on the railway in due course. Refreshments are available close to Ham Lane station. An interesting railway with very helpful staff. There are two extensive car parks close to Ham Lane station, a parking fee applies.

*About 45 years ago this Dove 4-6-4 operated as No. 1951, **Commodore Vanderbilt**, on a line above Llandudno on the Great Orme. This view dated 1st July, 1979 shows the same engine arriving at Lynch station.*

It is interesting to compare this photograph of Dove 4-6-2 with the previous illustration. Note the changed cab, chimney and smoke deflectors. Nameplates had not been fitted. The transition from **Commodore Vanderbilt** to **Henry** is quite remarkable. Photographed at Ham Lane station on 15th April, 1987.

Hunslet 0-4-0ST **Ivor** was jointly built by D. Jones/A. Mills in 1990. This locomotive is a useful addition to the railway, being changed over periodically with **Henry**. The illustration shows **Ivor** following cleaning and boiler washout outside the running shed. 19th July 1998.

How it all looks now. **Henry**, now a 4-6-2 and photographed near the South end of Lynch Lake, is equipped with new cylinders of 117mm bore; giving a welcome increase in tractive effort. The tender was rebuilt during 1997, making it more practical in use. 19th July 1998

Hastings Miniature Railway,   10¹/₄ inch.

Sea front, Hastings, East Sussex.

The formative days of this railway date back to around 1947 when it was owned by Capt.Howey for one season only. The Captain bought the LMS 4-6-0 *Royal Scot* from Lord Downshire's own railway at Easthampstead Park. Over the winter of 1947/8 the Scot was overhauled and the railway at Hastings was later purchased by Ian Allan. During the period of Capt.Howey's ownership the 8ft. express passenger tank of Great Northern appearance, a 4-4-2T No.175 that was built by George Francis Gabriel Des Vignes (1848-1935) in 1917, was tried at Hastings but dropped inside the track as it was only 10¹/₈th gauge! No. 175 returned to New Romney and has remained there ever since, displayed inside a glass case. It is possible the No. 175 indicated May, 1917. It is a complete locomotive but it is not known if this engine was ever steamed - a very early visiting engine to Hastings!

The other locomotives at Hastings were the GWR 4-6-0 No.2943 *Hampton Court*, now at *Stapleford Park Miniature Railway*, and the Bullock 0-6-0 No. 3007 *Firefly* (built as a Pannier Tank in 1936). At Hastings in the early 1960's No. 3007 carried a yellow livery and is now with *Kerrs Miniature Railway* at Arbroath, still in excellent condition. The Scot, built originally as No. 6100, was re-numbered post nationalisation to 46100 and moved on to *Oakhill Manor Railway* where a lengthy 10¹/₄ inch line opened to the public (now closed). It was last seen stored inside a warehouse at Dukinfield near Guide Bridge for several months awaiting shipment and has now emigrated to America. The Scot was built in 1938 to a Bassett-Lowke order by Messrs. J.Braunston & Walters. Hastings Miniature Railway still operates with a diesel locomotive.

*At Hastings, No. 46100 **Royal Scot** runs round its stock against a backcloth of wooden huts. A photograph from the archives of 1968.*

*The Hastings Miniature Railway, another view of **Royal Scot** on the beach about 30 years ago.*

Kerrs Miniature Railway.   10¹/₄ inch.

West Links, Arbroath, Angus.

Kerr's is an old established miniature railway dating back to 1935, operating first as a 7¹/₄ inch gauge for three years, when a decision was taken to increase the gauge to 10¹/₄ inch.

At West Links is a spacious locomotive shed and workshops; the station has three platforms linked by a footbridge. Outside the running shed are a turntable, signal box and some cosmetic signals. The railway extends ¹/₄ mile with an excellent track; trains operate from West Links smokebox first to Hospitalfield Halt, where there is a single platform, run round loop and turntable. Trains are generally propelled on the return journey.

Steam is used at weekends and at other times as required. Of particular interest is the former *Hastings Miniature Railway* Bullock 0-6-0 of 1936 No. 3007 **Firefly** now finished in a smart green livery. At Hastings she ran for some years painted yellow. A second Bullock engine of 1935 a 4-6-2 No.2005 **King George VI**, once named **Princess Marina** and later **Silver Jubilee** has been fully restored. The railway has a number of internal combustion locomotives, the most notable of which is No. 9872 **Auld Reekie**, a steam outline 4-4-2, built by W.L.Jennings in the 1930's, and powered by a petrol engine in the tender.

The attractive entrance to West Links station at Kerr's Miniature Railway. A nice viewpoint showing the platforms, signal box, footbridge and locomotive shed. 29th Jul9, 1994.

In 1994 Guest built LMS class 5 4-6-0 No. 5156 *Ayrshire Yeomanry* - in red livery, which had been on loan to Kerr's was sold and is now in private ownership (repainted black) in the South of England. One of Kerr's closed coaches No. 9138 is now also preserved on a private railway.

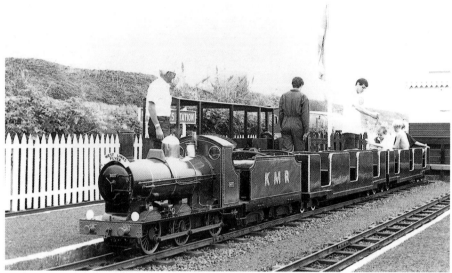

*0-6-0 No. 3007 **Firefly** waits at platform 3 at West Links station on 29th July, 1994.*

*Outside the shed at Arbroath was this red Guest Class 5 4-6-0 LMS No.5156 **Ayrshire Yeomanry** along with other locomotives on static display.*

*Arrival of an afternoon express from West Links hauled by **Firefly** at Hospitalfield Halt. 29th July, 1994.*
Photography by kind permission of the KMR Management.

Leek & Manifold Miniature Railway.

10¹/₄ inch.   (Annual Installation)

Hulme End, Staffordshire.

The Leek & Manifold Miniature Railway was unusual in being a temporary line which first operated in 1984 and was subsequently relaid each season. It was used about two or three weekends in June, the 10¹/₄ inch gauge track laid on the original 2ft. 6inch gauge alignment of the former *Manifold Valley Light Railway*, now a pedestrian walkway and pony trail.

Early operation at Hulme End began with a Leek & Manifold 2-6-4T No.2 *J.B.Earle* built by the late D.Blackhurst and based on Kitson No. 4258 of 1904. Trains ran from Hulme End, propelling outwards for about ¹/₂ mile as required. Cosmetic signals were placed at suitable locations to provide a railway atmosphere. By June, 1990 *J.B.Earle* was replaced by two new 2-6-4T's by the same builder, finished in maroon livery. They were No.1 *Manifold* and No.2 *Dove*, both had combined name and builders plates, dated 1990.

By the 1990 season the railway had reached Apes Tor, out of sight of Hulme End; the same method of propulsion being used. Both engines were in steam, servicing being carried out between trips at Hulme End. The ride was free but a collection box was placed at a strategic location, donations going to a preferred charity. The *Leek & Manifold Miniature Railway* service terminated in 1993.

It is interesting to mention that three L&M locomotives have been built in miniature, *E.R.Calthrop* (Colby Simkins Engineering Ltd) in 1974, *J.B.Earle* (both 10¹/₄ inch locomotives), and 12¹/₄ inch gauge *Fairbourne & Barmouth Railway Elaine,* later to lose its identity to become *Russell* of the *Welsh Highland Railway*.

Both the L&M 10¹/₄ inch gauge locomotives worked together at Kessingland for a special weekend event in July, 1984. *E.R.Calthrop* is currently at Trago Mills and was transferred from its former home when the locomotive stock moved away from Suffolk Wildlife Park at Kessingland. *J.B.Earle* was offered for sale by a private owner during 1999.

Leek & Manifold 2-6-4T No.2
J.B.Earle *is seen here returning to Hulme End. Note the fixed distant signal. 16th June, 1984.*

Below:

Lunch break at Hulme End. **Manifold** *and* **Dove** *(nearest to the camera) simmer for a few minutes before working the next trip to Apes Tor. This railway was very popular with the visitors and even on a temporary track the ride was quite smooth. 17th June, 1990.*

Also shown on this page is an actual poster of the Manifold Light Railway when it was originally opened on Wednesday, 29th June, 1904 and of the Leek & Waterhouses Omnibus service of that era.

Littlestone-On-Sea Miniature Railway.

10¹/₄ inch.   Littlestone, Kent.

This 10¹/₄ inch gauge railway was operated by Colonel R.B.Tyrrell on the sea front at Littlestone, just over ³/₄ of a mile from New Romney station of the *Romney, Hythe & Dymchurch Railway*. It was a straight out and back ride, with the locomotive shed situated at the Dungeness end of the line and was around 400 yards in length.

It operated for several years in the mid - 1950's, starting with a Carland **Royal Scot** with open coaches, and later this locomotive was replaced with an Atlantic No. 1001 **Sir A. Montgomery**. This 4-4-2 was built by G&S Light Engineering Co. Ltd., in 1937 and became No. 1001 at *Dudley Zoo Railway* the following year. It has worked at many different locations and came to Littlestone from a private railway at North Tawton. Col. R.B.Tyrrell had previously operated a 10¹/₄ inch gauge railway at Dymchurch using the same Carland Scot.

In 1934 Colonel Tyrrell operated the 7¹/₂ inch gauge *Romney Miniature Railway*, situated quite close to New Romney station of the *Romney, Hythe & Dymchurch Railway*. The line was ¹/₄ mile in length with a turntable at both ends. The engines were a 0-4-4T named **Atalanta**, built by the Colonel in 1934, he had also built a much earlier engine, a 4-4-0 named **Mighty Atom** about 1912.

*A pensive Colonel Tyrrell waits with his locomotive No. 1001 **Sir A.Montgomery** whilst a photographer records the scene at Littlestone-on-Sea. One of the few photographs existing of this railway, 25th March, 1956.*

Photo : G.A.Barlow, BEM

Lower Peover Fete   10¹/₄ inch.

Near Plumbley, Cheshire.   (Temporary event).

A superb LB&SC 0-6-0T No. 82 **Boxhill** was in use at the Lower Peover village fete during 1983. The locomotive was using a temporary track installed in a field close to the local village church. Note the removable white cab roof; reinstated for a photo stop! Little is known about this engine but it was probably built c1982. Few Terriers have been built in this gauge, there are however two others in private ownership in the South of England which, like **Boxhill**, sometimes appear at similar events.

*Occasionally a rare locomotive comes as a surprise. Here at the Lower Peover annual fete was a Terrier, No. 82 **Boxhill** operating on portable track. Summer 1983.*

Mull & West Highland Narrow Gauge Railway.

10¹/₄ inch.

Craignure, Isle of Mull.

The Mull & West Highland Railway opened in August, 1983, followed by the official opening ceremony on 22nd June, 1984. Most visitors to the railway will travel by Caledonian Macbrayne's ferry from Oban on the west coast of the Scottish mainland. They operate during the season every two hours from around 10 o'clock, returning from Craignure an hour later.

The railway station at Craignure is just a few minutes walk from the ferry terminal. From here the railway extends just over a mile to Torosay Castle. There is a half way crossing loop on the railway. The locomotive shed is on the right hand side of the line from Craignure.

Torosay Castle is partly under trees but there is a path leading from the platform towards the Castle, which is in a very pleasant location having well kept gardens and a tea room. Building this railway was no light task and many problems were encountered due to extra foundation work being necessary.

The railway has three steam engines; Curwen Atlantic built 1948, No.196, (the former 2005) *Waverley*, 2-6-4T *Lady of the Isles;* R.Marsh 1981 and a 2-6-2T named *Victoria* built by David Vere, completed in 1993. Also there is a petrol and one diesel locomotive. At Craignure station there is a souvenir shop and booking office. The journey is very pleasant and the staff are most helpful.

*2-6-2T **Victoria** looked very smart in her blue livery. Here it is an excellent viewing point to see the arrival from Oban of the noon sailing of Caledonian MacBrayne's MV **Isle of Mull**. Craignure, 23rd September, 1993.*

Opposite: *Between Craignure and Torosay is a crossing point where there are water facilities if required and a good viewing point of the Sound of Mull. **Lady of the Isles** was working the service train on 17th August, 1984.*

The Narrower Gauge Railway   10¹/₄ inch.

Eirias Park, Colwyn Bay.

During the summer of 1991 a miniature steam railway returned to Colwyn Bay on the west side of Eirias Park using a ¹/₄ mile temporary alignment. There was one steam locomotive, a 2-4-4T named **Lynton**, originally built by Narogauge Ltd at Christchurch as a 7¹/₄ inch modified Tinkerbell No.8/1984. The locomotive was regauged to 10¹/₄ inch by David Yates in 1990. Eirias Park is rather hilly and it was quite surprising to find a railway at this location. The park is often very busy during the afternoons; in 1991 the railway was booked to open until 8th September. Locomotive and stock were stored inside a large shed each evening and re-railed the following day. A booking office issued travel tickets. The train initially was an out and back operation, running as required.

From July 1992 a permanent location was established for the railway. A fare of £1 applied for the ¹/₄ mile journey. The new alignment formed a circular route allowing a panoramic view of the North Wales main line and the Irish sea. Of particular interest was a RAIL CYCLE, this unusual machine, described as a Quadricycle, built by Crowhurst Engineering of Hythe in 1989 to 7¹/₄ inch gauge, was a track testing vehicle being regauged to 10¹/₄ inch by Yates of Blaenau Ffestiniog the following year. By 1996 the railway had closed, locomotive and stock being utilised at Gloddfa Ganol for a short time. **Lynton** was then sold to a private owner in Surrey and now operates on the *Little Giant Railway* at Merton, London.

*2-4-4T **Lynton** worked the railway at Colwyn Bay for a few years. This view shows the engine working on the first of the two layouts in Eirias Park on 20th August, 1991. This locomotive had worked previously on portable track at several locations including Llandudno. It had also worked at the Port Sunlight Centenary in 1988.*

Newby Hall Miniature Railway.   10¼ inch.

Newby Hall, Ripon, North Yorkshire.

The Newby Hall railway opened in April, 1971 and extends about 1000 yards taking visitors from the station on a pleasant journey around part of the extensive garden area. The line is formed of two loops, a centre section with a spur to the shed. The immaculate steam locomotive is a 4-6-0 LMS No. 6100 **Royal Scot** built by Stanley Battison of Ilkeston in 1953; also a Severn-Lamb diesel. The Scot normally operates on Sundays. An entrance fee is payable to visit the grounds.

*A specially posed "rods down" picture of the immaculate Newby Hall 6100 **Royal Scot** at the end of the day's running. 23rd July, 1989.*

North Midland Railway.   10¼ inch.

Loughborough, Leicestershire.

Running during 1973 at the *Great Central Railway* main line station was a 10¼ inch gauge miniature railway which operated alongside the up platform. It was a single line that extended northwards to a point beyond the length of the platform. The motive power was a Curwen Atlantic No.196 **Waverley** fully restored and renumbered from 2005, the number carried at Weymouth. This locomotive was purchased direct from Jack Doyle in Manchester. The railway closed and the locomotive was sold to the *Mull & West Highland Narrow Gauge Railway*, at Craignure.

*An unusual place to find a 10¼ inch gauge locomotive in steam! The North Midland Railway provided some excitement with a rebuilt Curwen 4-4-2 No. 196 **Waverley** on display at Loughborough GC station on 22nd July, 1973.*

Oakhill Manor Railway.   10¹/₄ inch.

Oakhill, near Bath, Somerset.

The ³/₄ mile Oakhill Manor Railway (owned by Mr. W.Harper) was situated in the grounds of the Manor, and was officially opened on 16th July, 1978 by Robin Leigh-Pemberton. A car park was provided adjacent to Grand Junction station, where visitors were transported to the Manor House. The line had extensive architectural features formed from Mendip stone; with a high level bridge over the railway. It had stations at Sunnyside for the picnic area and Loco Manor, the line passed over the lawn within sight of the house. Another station existed known as 'The Woodland Station' but this was not used in normal passenger operation. It was an ideal location for a miniature railway within easy reach of Bath, Cheddar, and Glastonbury.

Generally photographic possibilities were good. The railway had five steam locomotives, usually two would be operating when the line was open. The steam locomotives were 4-6-0 No. 46100 **Royal Scot** once owned by the Marquess of Downshire before the war, and a 1947 built David Curwen Pacific No. 2647 **Robin Hood**. The latter operated previously on occasions at the *Audley End Railway* but it was a privately owned engine.

A Hunslet 0-4-0ST, built 1977 by Richards Engineering of North Wales named **Nelly** was a regular engine, and new to the railway by 1979 was a Southern King Arthur 4-6-0, also built by Richards Engineering. This locomotive was finished in SR green livery but was then unnamed and carried no number. It is understood it became No. 772 **Sir Percivale**. A new GWR 2-8-0 47xx Class, No. 4700 built in 1983 also came to the line from miniature locomotive engineer Keith Wilson. A rake of Southern green liveried scale coaches and an open set were used. The railway sadly closed in 1988.

King Arthur 772 **Sir Percivale**, *here unlettered, stands at Oakhill Manor awaiting its next tour of duty, 27th August, 1979. A similar locomotive, 771* **Sir Sagramore** *was owned by the late Peter Howard, in Kent. It is now in private ownership.*

*The railway at Oakhill Manor is no longer operational. In its heyday its future seemed promising; it certainly attracted considerable numbers of visitors at weekends. This photograph shows 0-4-0ST **Nelly** running tender first 1978.*

Orchard Farm Holiday Village.   10¹/₄ inch.

Hunmanby, North Yorkshire.

A rather nice 10¹/₄ inch miniature railway opened in June, 1995 at Orchard Farm which is at the extremity of Hunmanby and only a short drive from Filey. Here a very attractive station has been built adjacent to the lake and the nearby caravan park.

The railway is about ¹/₃rd of a mile in length; from the station it passes over a level crossing, beneath a footbridge and beyond is a trailing connection to the locomotive shed. Here there are watering facilities, a turntable and three shed roads. The line continues on a right hand curve through a tunnel and in cuttings; rejoining the same track then passing the outside of the station building around the lake to the platform. A second road here is used for locomotive purposes. The railway had an LMS No. 6100 **Royal Scot** (now sold) and a Great Northern Atlantic **Sir Walter Gower**. There is also an Inter-City DH locomotive named **Honeywell**. The steam situation was under review at the time of writing. It is an interesting railway on a pleasant site.

*LMS 4-6-0 **Royal Scot** waits for a turn of duty on the Orchard Farm Railway on 27th August, 1995. Note the high reflected light from the new ballast.*

*On the Orchard Farm Railway GN Atlantic **Sir Walter Gower** is a locomotive unseen by many, although its history is documented for over a quarter of a century. On this occasion the 4-4-2 was due to work a goods train during the early afternoon of 27th August, 1995.*

Royal Victoria Railway. 10¹/₄ inch.

Royal Victoria Country Park, Netley, Southampton.

*A specially posed picture of Curwen 2-6-0 No.4 **Isambard Kingdom Brunel** on the 10¹/₄ inch gauge Royal Victoria Railway, Netley. Quite a delightful setting in the late afternoon sunlight and within walking distance of Southampton Water. 14th August 1993.*

The first railway in the Royal Victoria Park was built to 10¼ inch gauge, it opened during 1989, had no official title and was totally dismantled by April, 1995.

The Royal Victoria Railway acquired the site on 1st May, 1995, operating a diesel service on 24th August the following year. In the summer of 1997 a steam and diesel service was introduced on Saturdays, as well as special event days.

The railway commences at Chapel Road station, a long single platform with a passing loop. From the station trains operate over a one mile circular route through woodlands, passing the stock shed at a higher level. Present motive power is a Curwen 2-6-0 No.4 *Isambard Kingdom Brunel*, a locomotive that worked at the *Crowlas Woodland Railway* in Cornwall twenty years ago. This engine was purchased by the present operator in dismantled condition, and has now been restored to working order.

The railway operates from 11.30/4.30pm, weekends and Bank Holidays, additionally during school holidays. The fare is £1.50 with usual reduction for children. A small DH machine is also available. There are good photographic locations lineside late afternoon. Refreshments can be obtained from a nearby café in the park. Parking facilities are pay and display.

The Special Train Staff at the Royal Victoria Railway.
Courtesy : Helen Allenby

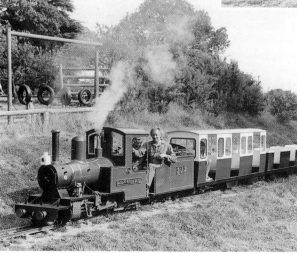

At the close of daily operation the locomotive and coaching stock are taken to the shed; this view shows No.4 - the original number at Crowlas - **Isambard Kingdom Brunel** *pausing for a moment close to the children's play area. On this occasion the Curwen was being driven by the railway's manager, Mr.Peter Bowers. 14th August, 1998.*

Rudyard Lake Railway.   10¹/₄ inch.

Near Leek, Staffordshire. (first railway on this site)

Rudyard Lake Railway was officially opened by the Hon. John Gretton on 27th June, 1978. The official train was hauled by Leek & Manifold 2-6-4T No.1, *E.R.Calthrop* built by Coleby Simkins Engineering Ltd, 1974. The locomotive was based on Kitson 4257/04 - one of the original L&M engines. Prior to this historic occasion the railway had been operating works trains on Sundays. Fares were 15p return; souvenir tickets were issued on the train and from a kiosk at Rudyard Lake.

The railway was laid on the left of the former BR alignment looking north (from the site of Rudyard Lake station) to a point near the south end of the lake where a platform was installed. Initially the locomotive faced north but operated facing south for the official train as photographic possibilities were improved. The railway was installed by Brian Nicholson and his son, David.

Initially there were no stock sheds and locomotive and coaches were removed from the site after the last train of the day. The engine fitted neatly inside a horse box! During the construction of the railway some track and two locomotives were recovered from a line at Prestatyn. A very good 10¹/₄ inch LMS 4-6-0 No. 6100 *Royal Scot,* built by Foden's of Sandbach, was also acquired. This railway, the first 10¹/₄ inch gauge line at Rudyard Lake was removed to a new location at Kessingland Wildlife Park near Lowestoft in 1980.

The opening of the line attracted a number of visitors and local people. Here, a youthful Bob Moore was honoured to take invited guests from the vicinity of the Lake to the end of the railway which was nearer to the site of former BR Rudyard Lake station. 27th June, 1978.

E.R.Calthrop was the locomotive normally in service on the first railway. In this view of 13th May, 1979, the weather was good and it was a popular journey. The driver on this occasion was the late Mr. Brian Nicholson.

Rudyard Lake Railway.   10¹/₄ inch.

Near Leek, Staffordshire. (second railway on this site)

The existing railway at Rudyard Lake is the second 10¹/₄ inch gauge line to be constructed on this alignment and the third railway at this site, the rail bed of the former North Stafford/ LMSR North Road - Leek branch, closed to passenger traffic on 7th November, 1960 and to freight on 15th June, 1964. The present railway is installed on the right hand side of the track bed as viewed looking north from the site of the former BR station. It was opened in stages during 1985 following construction the previous year. The railway is operated by Mr. P. Hanton and is about 1¹/₂ miles in length; the line commences opposite the old station where there is a turntable and stock shed.

There are two steam locomotives, Bullock 4-4-0 *Ivanhoe* of 1937 that earlier in its history had worked at *Kerr's Miniature Railway* at Arbroath as 3009, and No.6 named ***River Churnet*** a 2-4-2T built by *Exmoor Steam Railway*, their 294 of 4/1993. The railway has a passing loop at Lakeside station, the journey terminating at Hunthouse Wood where there is another stock shed and turntable. The latter point is at the end of a delightful trip along the edge of the lake; the trains operating every 40 minutes, normally steam worked on Saturdays in the season. At other times diesels may be utilised. On Rudyard Lake there is a wood burner named ***Swan*** that sails from a landing stage on the opposite side of the lake offering a cruise at moderate cost. She was in use during May, 1994. The railway was advertised for sale in May, 1999.

*The first steam locomotive was 4-4-0 **Ivanhoe**; in this view at Lakeside, it is ready to proceed towards Rudyard Lake. Nowadays, 2-4-2T **River Churnet** is likely to operate the Saturday passenger trains. 22nd July, 1989.*

Shibden Miniature Railway. 10¹/₄ inch.

Shibden Park, Halifax, West Yorkshire.

The Shibden Miniature Railway is located in the park and within easy reach of the A58 south west of Halifax. The station is called Shibden Halt where there is a booking office, tunnel and stock shed. The steam locomotive is a red 0-6-0ST *Ivor* built by Brian Taylor in 1984 and there is one petrol locomotive. The railway is approximately a ¹/₂ mile circuit passing through woodlands and it is normally steam worked at weekends. There are three passenger coaches. The immediate vicinity of the railway is quite open and there are good photographic possibilities. It is a pleasant park with car parking facilities.

The delights of Shibden Park! 0-6-0ST Ivor makes light work of the pleasant journey through the woodlands. October 1986.

Southend Miniature Steam Railway.

10¹/₄ inch.   Southend, Essex.

A ¹/₄ mile railway opened in July, 1977, using a green liveried 2-4-2 No.100 *Viking*, built by Viking Locomotives in 1977 which operated until 1982 around a circuit of the boating lake which is in the proximity of the famous pier. There was also a 4wBE and a 4w-4PM. *Viking* is now in private ownership. The railway closed at the end of 1985.

2-4-2 No.100 Viking simmering alongside the Boating Lake, Southend on 9th July, 1978.

Stapleford Miniature Railway.   10¹/₄ inch.

Stapleford Park, Melton Mowbray, Leicestershire.

The Earl of Northesk opened the Stapleford Miniature Railway on 18th May, 1958. It was operated by two Curwen Atlantics, No.750 **Blanche of Lancaster** and No.751 **John of Gaunt**, (originally 5748 and 2448). The original line commenced at Stable Hill station, close to a car park west of Central station and the first section to be lifted.

Central station was a terminal with three platforms, signal box and electrically illuminated lower quadrant signals. The locomotive running sheds and turntable were adjacent to the well constructed terminal station which had mains lighting for night running. From Central station the railway was run as two single lines, the left hand track went to the site of the present terminal station; (known as Lion Reserve Station) operating as a shuttle service bringing passengers for the boat train. The right hand running line tended to use the larger engines which hauled the boat train down to the lakeside.

North of Central station was a road crossing with lifting barriers. The line proceeded in a northerly direction to swing sharp right on to the present route and through Box tunnel to Lakeside station. This was an excellent vantage point for photography where the train engines could be seen simmering in the sunlight. At Lakeside the two boats **S.S. Northern Star** (Curwen & Newbury) or **S.S. Southern Cross** (Severn Lamb) would take passengers around the lake.

The railway was later extended from Lakeside station through the fields and back alongside the edge of the lake, rejoining at a point beyond the former Lakeside station site; now demolished.

*The Berkshire 2-8-4 No.752, then named **The Lady Margaret**, at the bottom of the bank having just left Lakeside station. To the right of the illustration is the lakeside.*

Sadly, two years after the unfortunate closure of the railway in 1982 Central station too was demolished, and the twin single line section severed. One of the two boats went for scrap, and the other was sold, its whereabouts not known. They were unique, powered by Ford engines and immensely popular. Who knows, perhaps one day, we may see a steamer return to the lake.

The present locomotive stock comprises 4-4-2 No. 751 *John.H.Gretton* (renamed), 4-6-0 LMS No. 5565 *Victoria*, 4-6-0 GWR No. 2943 *Hampton Court*, 2-8-4 Berkshire No. 752 (name removed), and 4-6-2 Nord 3.1192 (N.Simkins). 4-8-4 New York Central No. 6019 was inside the running shed during October, 1997. A visitor the same year was 4-6-2 LNER A4 No. 4498 *Sir Nigel Gresley,* built by W.Kirkland and used previously at Thoresby Hall. The Berkshire 2-8-4 was formerly named *The Lady Margaret*; she measured 18ft. 9 in. and was too long to fit on Central turntable. During the late 1970's a superb 6100 *Royal Scot* was on loan to the railway from a private owner in Norfolk. A 0-6-2T *Kingsley* had been test run on the railway in 1976; the engine went to *Age of Steam* and later to *Watford Miniature Railway* at Cassiobury Park. The railway now opens on two days each year. No doubt there are yet more surprises is store!

A photo stop at Stapleford Park; here Jubilee No. 5565 **Victoria** *has just caught the late afternoon sun, the wheels fully illuminated and rods down!*
19th August, 1978.

During August, 1976 this immaculate LMS 4-6-0 No. 6100 **Royal Scot** *was on loan to the railway. By special request she was positioned on the curve which was then the main line, for photography. Something to be said for persevering! The Scot was a privately owned engine from the Eastern Counties.*

*Curwen 4-4-2 No. 751 **John of Gaunt** (later renamed) pauses for the camera along the lakeside. The driver was the late John Gretton, a kind man who enjoyed driving on his railway.   19th August, 1978.*

*An early view of Curwen No. 750 **Blanche of Lancaster** emerging from beneath the vehicle crossing. This locomotive was sold from Stapleford Park to a new owner in Yorkshire, later it was purchased for use at Kessingland. 27th July, 1969.*

*A feature of Stapleford Park was the lake. Until the railway was extended all trains ran to Lakeside station where passengers could alight for the boat. Here is one of the two boats, **Northern Star**; set against a background of the island.   27th July, 1969.*

Ce qu'une très bonne idée! Bâtissant une machine à vapeur pour ce chemin de fer.
C'est excellent! Félicitations! (NORD 3.1192) Photographie 26.8.1995.
Truly one of the most magnificent machines built in recent years, the work of N.Simkins
and his son, completed in 1995.

*Curwen No. 751 **John of Gaunt**. A specially posed shot taken on the remaining section of the spur from Central station, 26th March, 1978.*

*Stapleford Park shed. This was situated alongside Central station. No. 750 **Blanche of Lancaster** was being prepared for the day's running. Now it is all history; this end of the railway was demolished. c.1968.*

*The recently completed 4-8-4 No. 6019 (**Niagara**) built by John Wilks. She operated normal service trains and is seen here on 30th August, 1998 returning to the junction alongside the lake. A superb machine and a valuable addition to the railway, and a great credit to her builder. With other 10¼ inch gauge locomotives in the pipeline Stapleford Park is now a miniature railway with an excellent future.*

*An interesting study of New York Central 4-8-4 No. 6019 (**Niagra**) ready to depart from Stapleford Park; photographed on the second open weekend during 1998, still well supported by the number of visitors present, some for their first time.*

*An end of season landscape in a Lakeland setting. LNER A4 Pacific **Sir Nigel Gresley** draws towards the colour light signal at Stapleford Park on 12th October, 1997.*

*An unusual engine to find at Stapleford Park is Great Western Railway 'Saint' 4-6-0 No. 2943 **Hampton Court** originally built by G&S Engineering in 1939. This engine worked for many years at Hastings Miniature Railway along with Nos. 46100 and 3007. It is in regular use on open days providing interesting photographic possibilities piloting other Stapleford locomotives.*

Suffolk Miniature Light Railway.   10¹/₄ inch.

Kessingland, Near Lowestoft.

This extensive 10¹/₄ inch gauge railway opened in 1980. It had one covered station with booking and other facilities; here all trains commenced their journey radiating round a large field. The railway was well planned having two loops, over bridge and cuttings - the system was fully signalled on a computer control system.

Initial locomotive stock was transferred from *Rudyard Lake Miniature Railway*; these were the Coleby Simkins Engineering Ltd 2-6-4T No.1 **E.R.Calthrop** based on *Leek & Manifold Valley Railway* Kitson 4257/04, and LMS 4-6-0 No. 6100 **Royal Scot** built at Foden's at Sandbach. One of the ex-*Stapleford Park Miniature Railway* Curwen Atlantics No.750 **Blanche of Lancaster** (the blue one) was purchased after outdoor storage for some years in the Sheffield area and was restored to working order at Kessingland.

During 1984 a 2-6-0 named **Alice** was supplied by (quote from plate) Simkins & Vere - Makers of Amusing Machinery, 1984. Four of the steam locomotives moved to the *Bickington Steam Railway*, the Scot was later sold to a private line in Suffolk. The Curwen 4-4-2 was originally No. 5748.

The Railway has since closed and the track has now been lifted. The surviving diesel hydraulic 4w+4w **Conway Castle** built by Fenlow Products c.1971 moved to the *Watford Miniature Railway*. **Rhuddlan Castle** had also moved with the steam allocation to the *Bickington Steam Railway*.

The shed at Kessingland housed this really nice looking 6100 **Royal Scot** *- the only known miniature locomotive built at Foden's. 2nd April, 1983.*

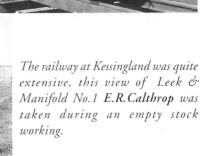

The railway at Kessingland was quite extensive, this view of Leek & Manifold No.1 **E.R.Calthrop** *was taken during an empty stock working.*

Good use had been made of the Kessingland site. Here No. 750 **Blanche of Lancaster** *after full restoration came back into service with a new boiler and partial repaint. Note the tender lettering referring to her ownership some years earlier at Stapleford Miniature Railway where she returned albeit as a visitor during August, 1995.*
11th May, 1986.

Syon Park Miniature Railway. $10^{1}/_{4}$ inch.

Syon Park, Brentford, Middlesex.

The miniature railway at Syon Park opened in 1993. It is situated just a short distance from the house, but within its extensive grounds, for which there is an entrance fee payable. The first section was almost a straight track with a spur to the engine shed.

The first locomotive was LMS streamlined Pacific No. 6220 **Coronation**, built by Ernest Dove in 1946. This engine had previously worked at the *Christchurch Miniature Railway* where there was a short circle of track. Later, a Carland Scot No. 6100 **Royal Scot** arrived which was originally at *Dymchurch Miniature Railway* and then *Littlestone Miniature Railway* in Kent. The railway has since been extended nearer to the house. The extension was open by June 1994 when 0-6-0 No.4179 **Chiltern Shuttle** was a visiting engine from *Watford Miniature Railway*.

Thoresby Hall Railway.   10^{1}/$_{4}$ inch.

Near Ollerton, Nottinghamshire.

The railway at Thoresby Hall was on an almost straight alignment worked by W.Kirkland's 4-6-2 LNER A4 No. 4498 *Sir Nigel Gresley*. Passengers boarded from a wooden decked platform set on sleepers. The length of the line was about 400 yards, worked on the pull push method, smokebox first from the platform. Near the end of the journey the train passed through a timber building which doubled as a stock shed. During June, 1968 the A4 was in LNER green livery which later gave way to blue. After a period out of use No.4498 has been restored and was in use at *Stapleford Park Miniature Railway* on 12th October, 1997.

There was a 7^{1}/$_{4}$ inch railway quite close to Thoresby Hall at Ollerton Cross Roads where W.Kirkland's 4-6-2 A3 *Flying Scotsman* and/or 4-6-2 A2 *Earl Manvers* operated on Sundays. In the late 1980s the Hall was sold to the National Coal Board and the line subsequently closed due to subsidence.

It is now over thirty years ago that LNER A4 Pacific No. 4498 **Sir Nigel Gresley** *found a home at Thoresby Hall! The driver was busy collecting his fares from a temporary platform. A view from the archives of 1968.*

Opposite : *The only Dove streamlined Pacific, No. 6220* **Coronation***. When the railway at Syon Park opened the line was much shorter than it is nowadays. This photograph was taken about half way along the present formation towards the shed on 4th December, 1993. This locomotive had previously operated around a circuit at Christchurch.*

The Towans Railway. 10¹/₄ inch.

Near St.Ives Bay, Hayle, Cornwall.

The Towans Railway opened in June, 1972 and it was situated close to Riviere Estate Chalet Camp. It was within easy reach of the A30. The railway had a station, 40ft. tunnel along with cuttings and a footbridge, typical of many seaside miniature railways. It did have one steam locomotive, a LMS Compound 4-4-0 No.1070. This is a most interesting locomotive having been built, probably in 1928, to 9¹/₄ inch gauge.

Its pedigree is uncertain; some publications have credited Bassett-Lowke with construction but expert opinion does not share this view. It was for many years owned by R. Horsfield, E.D., A.M.I.Mech.E., M.I.Loco.E. and used on the *Indian Midland Railway* at Jhansi during the early 1930's as LMS No.1102. An article published in July, 1935 by Mr. Horsfield does not mention the locomotive's construction and the possibility exists that the Compound might have been built outside the UK. The Compound left India in 1946 and is known to have worked at Hunstanton Pier from c.1947 to 1959. In later years it became No. 41199 in line with the 1948 *British Railways* image. The plate on the engine indicates "Built Derby 1928". The standard gauge Compound LMS No. 1102 was built at Derby in October, 1925, and withdrawn by BR in December, 1958. It is therefore possible that No.1070 was built in 1928.

In late 1979, No.1070 (as it was then numbered) was kept in a narrow shed at Hayle and pulled outside on a rope for photography. Beyond, at the rear of the Compound, was a battery operated Carland Scot. No.1070 had a 17A shed plate (Derby) and carried the name **Maid Marion.** At this time No.1070 cosmetically looked very smart and seemed well looked after; some early photographs at Towans showed the engine in steam. Later, the engine was sold from the site and stored elsewhere out of use, to be offered for sale at Christie's Auction on 24th February, 1994 and following purchase it is now at Watford. The Towans Railway has since closed.

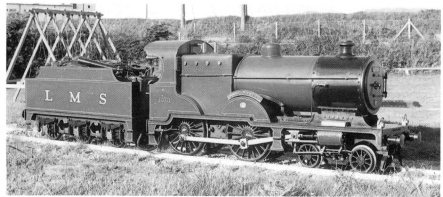

*LMS Compound No. 1070 **Maid Marion** still looking immaculate, stands outside the shed at the Towans Railway, Hayle on 22nd August, 1979.*

Watford Miniature Railway.   10¹/₄ inch.

Cassiobury Park, Watford, Hertfordshire.

Watford Miniature Railway was opened at Easter, 1959, on a site leased from Watford Borough Council, by Mr.C.H.Reed of Watford. It was steam worked using LMS Compound 4-4-0 No.41199, originally built to 9¹/₄ inch gauge in 1928 and used initially on a garden railway owned by Mr.R.Horsfield at Jhansi in India. When new the LMS 4-4-0 was No.1102. The Jhansi Railway was a ¹/₄ mile circuit, fully signalled; it had two main stations, at Dilkusha Terminus and Kaisar Bagh; the railway known as the *Indian Midland*. Whilst at Watford as No. 41199 the Compound was named ***Maid Marion***.

In 1979 Mr. Jeff Price became owner and operator and considerably enlarged the layout. The railway has an extensive terminal station where all trains commence their journey. The line leaves the station on a long left hand curve; passing a gate crossing to enter a restricted area of woodlands. Here there are two wide loops; both are traversed in a run of 1000 yards before returning to the station, the locomotive then being turned and prepared for the next journey.

There are three regular engines normally available, American Switcher 0-6-0 No. 4179 ***Chiltern Shuttle*** built during early 1940's by R.H.Morse, 2-6-0 No. 7 ***Marri***, the latter

On the turntable at Cassiobury Park, 18th September, 1993 was this very attractive locomotive 2-6-0 No.7 Marri an import to Britain from Australia.

*No. 4179 **Chiltern Shuttle** is approaching the station on the Watford Miniature Railway at Cassiobury Park on 24th September, 1989.*

built at Riverdale, Perth, Western Australia as 46/1993 by Willis Light Engineering Company, and *Conway Castle*, a Bo-Bo diesel hydraulic.

Marri is unique as she was transported by air freight from Perth by a British Airways Boeing 747 passenger aircraft on Thursday, 6th May, 1993. The aircraft arrived at Heathrow on Friday,7th May and the locomotive was collected by Mr. Price from the Cargo Terminal at 0130 hours on Saturday! The engine and tender were in their own crates, taken to Watford and *steamed* the same day for the Boiler Inspector!

Mr. Price's first steam locomotive was GNR Atlantic No.4442, built by A.J.Glaze in May, 1961, which ran here from 1983 until replaced by larger locomotives which followed. Another locomotive which moved from Watford in 1997 was 0-6-2T *Trevithick*; built by Minimum Gauge Railways as No.80/1975. When new it was named *Kingsley* and trials were carried out at *Stapleford Park Miniature Railway* during 1976, later moving to *Age of Steam*, Cornwall , prior to entering service at Watford in 1987.

0-6-2T Trevithick worked for a period on the Watford Miniature Railway. It is shown here when brand new at the Stapleford Miniature Railway as Kingsley in 1976.

Wells Harbour Railway.   10¹/₄ inch.

Wells-next-the-sea, Norfolk.

The railway at Wells is close to the harbour where Wells Town station is to be found. The line extends from here to the caravan site and sea where it terminates at Pinewoods Central station, ⁷/₁₀th of a mile distant. In June, 1979 the locomotive in use was a 0-4-2T named *Edmund Hannay* built by King of Norwich in 1971. Four open coaches are used.

A time table service operates at frequent intervals, including evening trains, from Easter onwards. In favourable weather conditions the rail connection is quite popular. The railway has turntables at both stations and was built and operated by Commander Roy Francis for some years after its opening in 1976. The railway also has a petrol locomotive called *Alfa*. A steam outline 0-6-0DH named *Densil* was delivered to the railway in July, 1998.

An interesting view of ***Edmund Hannay*** *which shows considerable detail of the construction of this engine. At Wells-on-Sea, 9th June, 1979.*

Wells & Walsingham Light Railway.

10¹/₄ inch.   Wells-next-the-sea, Norfolk.

The year 1982 marked the opening of the longest 10¹/₄ inch gauge railway in the UK. A short distance from the town is the starting point for the four mile journey to Walsingham. The railway is built on the track bed of the former *British Railways* Wells - County School (Great Eastern) branch line, which closed to passenger traffic on 5th October, 1964 and to all traffic on 2nd November of that year. It was a branch that operated some of the first Derby built diesel multiple units.

The present 10¹/₄ inch railway is single line with turntables at both terminals. It was worked initially by an 0-6-0T No.1 named ***Pilgrim*** - a name associated with the Shrine at Walsingham. The locomotive was built by D.H.King of Norwich in 1981. The railway now uses a 2-6-0 + 0-6-2 Garratt No. 3 ***Norfolk Hero*** built by N.Simkins in 1986. A diesel 6wDH is also used. Four or five journeys are made daily during the operating season.   ***Pilgrim*** has recently

Looking towards Wells-next-the-sea. Garratt No.3 ***Norfolk Hero*** *heads in the direction of Walsingham on 5th July, 1987.*

been purchased by the Wensleydale Railway Association along with three coaches and a quantity of rail. It is likely to be used at outdoor events with portable track. One to watch out for!

A late afternoon photograph at Wells of the Wells & Walsingham Light Railway Garratt No.3 **Norfolk Hero**. *This smart looking machine was preparing to run round its train. 5th July, 1987*

Before the Garratt came to the Wells & Walsingham Railway **Pilgrim** *worked the line. This view shows the Walsingham terminal of the railway, the train now ready to return to Wells. 1st April, 1983.*

Chapter 4
$9^1/_2$ & $8^1/_4$ inch Gauge

$9^1/_2$ inch

Astle Park

Bressingham Garden Railway

Burton Constable Hall Miniature Railway

Embsay Miniature Steam Railway

Hall Leys Miniature Railway

Kings Arms Miniature Railway

Lakeshore Railroad

$8^1/_4$ inch

Bankside Miniature Railway

Beaulieu Gardens Railway

Astle Park, Chelford.   9¹/₂ inch.

Cheshire.   (Visiting Miniature Railway)

Astle Park has for many years been a venue for an annual weekend Traction Engine Rally, but it is not guaranteed to produce a miniature railway every time. It is however worth a visit as two different locomotives have appeared on previous occasions, both being 9¹/₂ inch gauge and comparatively quite rare nowadays. In 1971, Atlantic No. 3440 appeared from South Shields as a visitor. This locomotive was later rebuilt with an extra set of driving wheels and is now a Pacific with the *Lakeshore Railroad*, South Shields, Tyne & Wear.

In 1997 former *Southsea Railway* 1928 built Bassett-Lowke Atlantic No. 1442 **Sir Edward Nicholl** visited Chelford. It was bought new by Comdr. Sir Edward Nicholl, KCB, DL, JP. and used for a while on his private railway at Littleton Park, Shepperton. The same year **Sir Edward Nicholl** visited other traction engine events at Carrington, Lincs., Grappenhall, and Old Warden! Rides on the 9¹/₂ inch gauge were 50p. The future location of this rally is uncertain.

Atlantic No. 3440 **Mountaineer** *was working shuttle journeys on a short length of 9¹/₂ inch gauge track at Astle Park, Chelford, 15th August, 1971. By some coincidence 26 years later yet another 9¹/₂ inch gauge locomotive was in steam at the same site!*

Bressingham Garden Railway. 9¹/₂ inch.

Bressingham Steam Museum, Diss, Norfolk.

Becoming rather scarce nowadays are 9¹/₂ inch gauge railways. Bressingham had one until 1994 when the installation was removed and replaced by a 10¹/₄ inch system. The Garden Railway, which was a contiuous track of about ¹/₂ mile in length, only had one locomotive, a 4-6-2 named **Princess** built by Motor Gear and Engineering Co. in 1947 No.2003. She was sold in February, 1995 for use on a proposed 9¹/₂ inch miniature railway at the Midland Railway Centre. **Princess** was one of a pair, the other one, **Prince** was built by Severn-Lamb from MG&E castings in 1972, for a private owner. The replacement locomotive was built to 10¹/₄ in. gauge, named **Alan Bloom**. A second similar engine was built and has been sold. Bressingham also have a lengthy 15 inch gauge railway worked by two Krupp Pacifics (see page 60).

*The original Garden Railway at Bressingham only had one steam locomotive, Pacific No. 2003 **Princess**. This photograph of a quarter of a century ago was taken in the late afternoon of 26th August, 1973.*

Opposite : *This well kept Bassett-Lowke 9¹/₂ inch gauge 4-4-2 **Sir Edward Nicholl** was once a Southsea locomotive; and still has its Southsea Railway name plates. It was photographed on a temporary portable track at Astle Park, Chelford Traction Engine Rally on 9th August, 1997. The fare to ride was 50p. This locomotive operated at other similar events during that year.*

Burton Constable Miniature Railway.

9¹/₂ inch.   East Riding of Yorkshire.

(Burton Constable Hall is situated about ³/₄ mile north of B1238 at Sproatley).

This 9¹/₂ inch gauge railway opened c.1973 and was operating during 1977 on approximately 100 yards of straight track. Only one steam locomotive was known to have been used, an Atlantic named **Gloria** built in Northern Ireland in 1968.

She was very much freelance in appearance and bore a lined maroon livery with the railway's crest painted on the sides of the firebox, her name likewise displayed on the smoke deflectors. **Gloria** was housed inside a shed at the end of the line, operation was by pull-push, pulling outward and propelling back. There were few photographic locations due to a very close fence, but at the end of the day's running a gate could be opened and the locomotive positioned!

It was the original intention to relay the railway elsewhere within the grounds but **Gloria** was stored from 1977 when the line closed, until sold for use on a miniature railway at Whitworth Hall, near Spennymoor in 1992. The locomotive was sold again in 1994 to a private railway.

Embsay Miniature Steam Railway.   9¹/₂ inch.

Embsay, near Skipton, North Yorkshire.

A very short 9¹/₂ inch gauge railway operated during August, 1975. Motive power on this line was a 2-4-2 named **King Tut** and built by S.Smith in 1934. It was one of the locomotives in the collection of Capt. Vivian Hewitt in Anglesey. The track ran alongside a fence of the car parking area adjacent to the Embsay station site, now the *Embsay and Bolton Abbey Steam Railway.*

The engine carried a name plate on the smokebox door and had a six wheel tender. In more recent years **King Tut** was re-gauged to 7¹/₄ inch gauge and was at *Wellington Country Park Railway* in June, 1994. The miniature railway at Embsay was closed in September, 1983 and all traces removed by 1985.

*Opposite : **King Tut** was a very rare locomotive to find simmering away quite unexpectedly at the Embsay site on 3rd August, 1975. After the locomotive left the collection of Captain V.Hewitt it was discovered on a boat named **Ashby** on the quay at Caernarfon at the end of November, 1966.*

*The end of another day. Here, **Gloria** was positioned for this photograph before retiring to the shed, August, 1977*

Hall Leys Miniature Railway.   9¹/₂ inch.

Hall Leys Park, Matlock, Derbyshire.

The Hall Leys miniature railway opened in 1948. It was basically a 250 yard single line running close to the River Derwent. Three steam locomotives had been used on the railway, all Pacifics built by S. Battison at Ilkeston; one in 1947, another in 1948, and the final one in 1949. Identifying them was sometimes difficult. The 1947 engine is possibly in America though its precise whereabouts still remain unknown.

The 1948 locomotive received No. 6201; it was eventually sold and emerged as a static exhibit at Riber Castle. It was later to surface at an auction in Matlock and obtained for eventual use at the Midland Railway Centre. It is now stored there pending possible restoration. Both No. 6201 and the 1949 engine known as *Lady Joyce* were photographed on the same day during August, 1975.

At that time the 1949 locomotive carried no identity; but as only two Pacifics were here at that time it could not have been any other! Since then the 1949 Pacific has gone and, like the 1947 engine, is probably in America.   There were periods when the Matlock engines ran without any visible identity; they also moved about to some extent with the Matlock Bath line. The 1947 engine was numbered 1947; its tender lettered LNER. In 1974 a Coleby Simkins 6wDH *Little David* arrived at Hall Leys and steam working, retained for a while as standby, eventually came to an end.

*If ever there was confusion it was at Matlock. This photograph shows the 1949 built locomotive, once named **Lady Joyce**. Various liveries emerged over the years and some locomotive numerals were stick on labels. It is probable but unconfirmed, that this engine went to America.*

Very likely this is the only Battison 9¹/₂ inch gauge Pacific left in this country. This is the 1948 engine, seen here as No. 6201 having received a cosmetic restoration at Riber Castle 23 years ago.

Kings Arms Miniature Railway.   9¹/₂ inch.

Public House, Cardington, Bedfordshire.

A short 9¹/₂ inch gauge railway existed here using an Atlantic named **Ruby** built by Parvers of Southport about 1914. The railway opened in 1962 in the grounds of the public house. The locomotive's livery was dark blue with brass boiler bands.

Trains were propelled outwards from the station; there was a trailing connection on the left to the locomotive shed and a tunnel along the curving formation. The railway survived for 20 years closing in 1982.

*Kings Arms Miniature Railway, Cardington. **Ruby** is already in steam and ready for service on this 9¹/₂ inch gauge railway. Note the delicate lining on the Atlantic's boiler and splashers. 27th August, 1973.*

Lakeshore Railroad.   9¹/₂ inch.

South Marine Park, South Shields, Tyne & Wear.

This railway opened in 1972 and it is one of the few built to the now unusual gauge of 9¹/₂ in. The line is a continuous 500 yard circuit around the boating lake. It once had a turntable that was part of the running line. The station has an island platform, with paved surface, allowing two train passenger loading, with an attractive canopy.

There are two steam locomotives sharing the duties, *Atchison, Topeka & Santa Fe* 4-6-2 No. 3440 **Mountaineer** rebuilt from an Atlantic during 1977, and a Colombian 2-6-2 No.27 **Adiela.** The Lakeshore Railroad was previously known as the *Ocean Park Railroad*.

> Opposite: *An interesting shot of Santa Fe 4-6-2 No. 3440 Mountaineer, seen here near the Sea Hotel at South Shields on 13th September, 1976. The illustration of this locomotive as an Atlantic can be seen under Astle Park, Chelford. (see page 122)*

Bankside Miniature Railway.   8¹/₄ inch.

Brambridge Park Garden Centre,
Kiln Lane, Eastleigh, Hampshire.

Brambridge station is the starting point of this most unusual miniature railway. It was built to 8¹/₄ inch gauge, operating on elevated track for a distance of 220 yards. Motive power is a 2-6-2T No.815 **Carolyn,** built in Basingstoke about 1924. The present owner has operated this locomotive every season since 1960, visiting Beaulieu on many occasions and Traction Engine Rallies, Carnivals and Fêtes over a wide area.

The late afternoon sunlight shows up the fine detail in this close up of 2-6-2T Carolyn, seen here at the conclusion of the weekend working. 15th August, 1998

Considerable work was undertaken on the locomotive including fitting new tyres, steel boiler, and many internal modifications have been carried out. The external appearance has been carefully maintained. **Carolyn** retains her smart maroon livery. Unfortunately, very little historical background is known about this exquisite locomotive.

Four passenger coaches are in use named *Diane, Marjorie, Maureen* and *Sylvia*. The railway is located at low level adjacent to the car park. The fare is 40p return, printed card tickets are issued from the Booking Office. An extension is currently being carried out on this unique line, it is truly a remarkable railway, the only known example of its kind and not one to be missed!

The Bankside Miniature Railway operates on a gradual right hand formation after leaving the station area. Here, a special photo stop was made to show the elevated 8¹/₄ inch gauge trackwork; the driver sits in his own designated compartment controlling **Carolyn** *from a seated position. Each passenger coach has its own name. Photographed on 15th August, 1998 with driver Mr. Peter Merritt.*

Beaulieu Gardens M.R.   8¹/₄ in.

Beaulieu, Hants.   (Montagu Motor Museum).

This miniature railway was a visiting installation operating on elevated track within the grounds of Beaulieu Gardens. The locomotive, a 2-6-2T No. 815 **Carolyn**, was built c1924 to the most unusual gauge of 8¹/₄ inch and was running here in the early 1960's.

The railway and **Carolyn** visited Beaulieu up to four times each year to attend various functions held at different sites. One site was adjacent to the standard gauge static railway display and was used over a three year period, with a 100 yard long railway in use. At other times a shorter 60 yard track sufficed at specific points of interest in the Palace Gardens, including the field where the Rolls Royce Rally was held. The railway was always removed after each weekend event.

Also, on outside display, at Beaulieu on standard gauge track was an ex-*Southern Railway* 4-4-0 No. 928/30928 **Stowe** and three Pullman Cars; the 4-4-0 was withdrawn by British Railways at the end of 1962, eventually moving to Eastleigh for restoration in 1973. When the restoration of the Schools was completed **Carolyn** was used at Eastleigh Works Open Day on 13th May, 1973, **Stowe** is now at Sheffield Park on the *Bluebell Railway*.

The railway has since been installed at Brambridge Park Garden Centre, Eastleigh, in 1976 and is still operated by the same owners. (See *Bankside Miniature Railway,* details under previous entry).

Simmering in the summer sunlight is this 8¹/₄ inch gauge 2-6-2T Carolyn at Beaulieu Gardens in this undated picture from the early sixties.

Chapter 5
7¼ inch Gauge

Belton House Miniature Railway

Bents Garden Railway & Centre

Brookside Miniature Railway

Conwy Valley Railway & Museum

Croxteth Park Miniature Railway

Dobwalls Family Adventure Park

Eastbourne Miniature Steam Railway

Echills Wood Railway

Finney Gardens Miniature Railway

Fort Belan Miniature Railway

Gorse Blossom Miniature Railway

Great Cockcrow Railway

Grosvenor Park Railway

Halton Miniature Railway

Hemsworth Water Park Railway

Hilcote Valley Railway

Hilton Valley Railway

Little Western Railway

Manor Park Miniature Railway

Moss Bank Park Railway

Myddle Wood Railway

Ollerton Cross Roads

Riverside Miniature Railway

Silloth Miniature Railway

Strathaven Park Miniature Railway

Sydney Arms Miniature Railway

The Railway Age

Thornes Park Railway

Trentham Gardens Miniature Railway

Walsall Steam Railway

Weston Park Railway

Westby Miniature Railway

Willen Miniature Railway

Worden Park Railway

Belton House Miniature Railway. 7¹/₄ inch.

Near Grantham, Lincolnshire.

Belton House is a National Trust property on the A607 about three miles north of Grantham. The railway at Belton House opened in April, 1979 with a LNER A3 Pacific No. 4472 *Flying Scotsman* built in 1949 by A.L.Broadbridge. This locomotive had operated previously at Wyndham Park, Grantham until c.1978. The operating length of track is 500 yards and almost straight; trains reversed outwards and returned smokebox first. There is a loco shed; inside it in 1979 was 2-6-2 *Mountaineer* from *Manor Park Railway*, Glossop, then partially dismantled; the present whereabouts of both locomotives is unknown. The railway is now worked by petrol locomotives.

A3 Pacific No. 4472 Flying Scotsman had a good head of steam but not with many passengers. 16th April,1979.

Bents Garden Railway & Centre. 7¹/₄ inch.

Glazebury, Lancashire.

A short 'L' shaped railway operated on this site at weekends; steam being used on Sundays. Two locomotives are known to have worked this line, a red open cab Hunslet 0-4-0ST named *Joanna* built by J.Martell 1978 was in use at the end of September, 1984 and Class 5 4-6-0 No. 44720 named *Alan*, noted in steam during mid-April, 1985. This locomotive was built by A.Aldred during 1972.

This seemed an excellent summer venue for a miniature railway at a very busy Garden Centre only a few minutes from the A580 East Lancashire Road.

The railway opened July, 1984 operating at the rear of the outdoor sales display area with a makeshift locomotive shed at the far extremity of the line; here an extension was planned but only the earth works were started. Stock comprised of two coaches which had bench type seating. Passengers joined the train at a paved area close to the edge of the lake; it was an out and back shuttle with a fare of 10p.   The track work was aluminium. The line did not survive very long and it ran for only three seasons, closing in 1986.

*A Class 5 4-6-0 No. 44720 named **Alan** was the duty locomotive at Bents Garden Centre on 14th April, 1985.*

Brookside Miniature Railway.   7¹/₄ inch.

Brookside Garden Centre, Poynton, Cheshire.
(located between Hazel Grove and Poynton on A523).

The first railway at Brookside Garden Centre was built in 1984 to 5 inch gauge; but was soon found to be too small for serious operation, taking into account the spiralling passenger numbers. The railway was reconstructed to 7¹/₄ inch gauge, the present layout was opened in July, 1989 and it extends within the physical length of the centre. It is a railway of great interest with steam working during the operating season on Sunday afternoons and Bank Holidays.

This railway has its own brochure listing the stock in some detail; but there are other points of interest too. The magnificent GWR style, four-platform station allows for two train operation and is unusual in also having two turntables, semaphore signals and a full size non-operational signal box. The latter was recovered from the former *Lancashire & Yorkshire Railway* Aughton Road crossing near Southport. The interior of the station waiting room is the home to a very fine railway museum containing a well laid out display with so much to see.

Once on board we leave the station following the periphery of the large car park, the line passes through a tunnel where there is a spur into both the locomotive sheds and maintenance workshop. These were built to a high standard complete with smoke vents. Beyond here are the bridge, heather gardens and the garden sales display area. Here the railway passes an ornamental pool, craft chalets and greenhouses before retracing its route to the station, which is electrically illuminated at night.

There are many railway totems, nameboards and information signs around the station area, and numerous period enamel advertising signs throughout the whole site. Also on static display, located close to the café/restaurant, is a standard gauge Barclay 0-4-0ST No.2226/ 1946, named **Katie**, which worked at the ICI factory at Huddersfield. Several locomotives operate on the $7^1/_4$ inch gauge railway; at the time of writing each engines turned at the end of the journey.

The flagship is a scale LMS 4-6-0 No. 6100 **Royal Scot** that originated in the Liverpool area and is now on display in the museum. Working locomotives include 0-4-2T No. 3 **Lady Pauline**, 0-4-0ST No. 9, **Siân**, 0-4-0ST **Catherine**, and 0-4-2T named **Princess**. 1997 saw a new LMS Class 5 4-6-0, No. 5428 built by the late Norman Whooler was added to stock.

Over the winter of 1998/9 earth works commenced allowing a further $^1/_4$ mile extension of the railway around the periphery of the entire site through the display area and gardens. The extension will feature a further tunnel and an operational automatic barrier level crossing. This endeavour will see this interesting line running for a short distance alongside the A523 Hazel Grove - Macclesfield Road, from where it will pass beneath the site entrance to terminate at the station.

'The Greatest Little Train in Cheshire'

*About to join the main line again, here, a four coach set hauled by 0-4-2T No.3 **Lady Pauline** was heading towards the station. 28th July, 1991.*

*This attractive 4-6-0 No. 6100 **Royal Scot** is unquestionably the star of Brookside Garden Centre; photographed on the running line on 4th August, 1993. This locomotive is sometimes on display in the museum building.*

Conwy Valley Railway & Museum.

7¼ & 15 inch.   Betws-y-Coed, Gwynedd.

The Museum at Betws-y-Coed was established in the 1970's and was purchased as a going concern by Mr.Colin M.Cartwright in 1986. It is on the site of the former *British Railways* Goods Yard adjacent to the present station operated by First North Western Trains. It is a museum with a working 7¼ inch railway. The museum houses a quantity of general railway related material, tickets, signs, photographs, the centre piece being a *British Railways* Pacific in 15 inch gauge, 70000 **Britannia**, initially steamed at TMA Engineering Ltd of Birmingham in June, 1988.(Works No.8733/87).

The Museum shop has much of interest to the visitor, books, cards and models, and outside is a ¼ mile 15 inch gauge electric tramway operating at 110 volts d.c. The 7¼ inch gauge miniature railway was opened in 1979 and has two Denver & Rio Grande 2-8-0's No. 402 **Shoshone** and No. 407 **Old Rube**; the former purchased from the now closed *Croesor Junction & Pacific Railway*, the latter came to the railway after initial service at *Walsall Steam Railway*. Both these locomotives were built by Milner Engineering Chester Ltd., of Chester. **Sian**,an 0-4-2ST, was built by K.Humphries 3/1988 and came to the railway in 1994. In addition there is a Union Pacific diesel Bo Bo 6641, with an 8 h.p. Honda petrol engine and a Swiss Crocodile 0-6-0 + 0-6-0 Battery Electric as RhB 403 **Prince of the Parsenn**.

The 7¼ inch gauge railway extends about ½ mile, worked via a computerised control system using colour light signals, lifting barriers, and bridges, operating in a fully landscaped environment. The 7¼ inch LMS 4-6-0 No. 6126 **Sans Pareil** vacated the museum during October, 1994 and was steamed prior to moving to a new home in Scotland.

Pacific No. 6201 **Princess Elizabeth** - the owner's first locomotive - from the *Walsall*

Steam Railway has been fully restored to working order; she is now on display at the museum and may see occasional passenger duty on special events days. The footbridge linking Railtrack's station platform is perhaps unique as it spans three different gauges, 7¼, 15 inch, and 4ft. 8½ inch! Very good on site catering facilities are available in the Buffet Coach. There is a convenient visitor car park alongside the museum building. A nominal entrance fee applies to enter the museum.

Two Denvers at work on the Conwy Valley Railway! No. 405 **Utah** *is seen here piloting sister engine No. 412 at work around the circuit. Both engines were privately owned. A number of these useful engines have been built, the 2-8-0's manage most curves.*

The prize exhibit inside the Conwy Valley Museum is the 15 inch gauge BR Pacific No. 70000 **Britannia***. This scale locomotive was completed by TMA Engineering of Birmingham and, to celebrate the event, invited guests were able to witness this fine engine in steam on a short demonstration track. Unfortunately, the day was dismal with frequent rain showers. This locomotive has on special occasions been seen in steam at the museum, but not on a regular basis. Photographed at TMA Engineering on 9th June, 1988.*

*LMS 4-6-0 No. 6126 **Sanspareil** had for a few years resided inside a glass case within the confines of the museum display area. But the time had arrived when this superb Scot was sold. On this occasion the private buyer had arrived from Scotland and No. 6126 was steamed. A few proving runs were carried out on the Conwy Valley Railway, and soon the locomotive was on its way to a new home. It has since been used at other events. 24th September, 1994.*

Croxteth Park Railway.   7¹/₄ inch.

Croxteth Hall & Country Park, Liverpool.

The railway at Croxteth Park opened in 1981. Croxteth Halt is the only station on this short railway. It is located to the left of the driveway approaching the hall.

The station has a booking office and overall roof. Trains operate in a clockwise direction passing through a short tunnel, allowing two runs of the circuit via a passing loop alongside the station where the next train will possibly be waiting.

The whole site is totally enclosed with a high mesh fence; line side photography is only possible on request. The hall provides a large free car park and it is about 1¹/₂ miles from the East Lancashire Road, A580.

Croxteth Halt.
*The locomotive on the right **Estelle** is waiting in the platform, whilst on the left is No. 3 **Dennis** about to pass on the through running line.*
29th May, 1982.

Dobwalls Family Adventure Park. 7¼ inch.

Dobwalls, Liskeard, Cornwall.

Certainly one of the finest 7¼ inch railways to be found anywhere. The signs say it all. Denver station; the exotic atmosphere of the two circuits, Wyoming Plains Division, Colorado Forest Division, Union Pacific Railroad, and Rio Grande. A journey over these lines and one can be completely disorientated!

After the ride there are good photographic locations providing it is possible to determine the route! There are superb bridges, viaducts and rock cuttings with adequate paths linking everything together and the locomotive shed is often a hive of activity; the main station is on a long gradual curve where the sight of a Big Boy is something beyond imagination!

The large engines are the obvious attraction. On a busy day Union Pacific Big Boy No. X4008 4-8-8-4 *William Jeffers* built by Severn Lamb in 1978 may be in use or 4-8-4 No.818 *Queen of Wyoming* Severn Lamb of 1974 and perhaps 4-8-4 No. 838 *Queen of Nebraska* also from Severn Lamb of 1981 as well. In addition there are several other engines which share the work of transporting excited passengers over this magnificent railway.

They are a 2-8-2 No. 488 *General Palmer* 1971, 2-6-2 No. 8 *David Curwen* 1972, and 2-8-2 No. 498 *Otto Mears* 1980, all built by David Curwen. Additionally there are four massive diesel locomotives reflecting American practice.

Union Pacific 'Big Boy' X4008 **William Jeffers** *is ready to depart from Denver station at Dobwalls; the young lady chatting to owner John Southern is the Guard.*
23rd August, 1979.

*The smaller engines at Dobwalls were also kept busy, a rare view of 2-6-2 No.8 **David Curwen** approaching the station.   23rd August, 1979.*

A compelling sign to read. Obviously a lot of thought went into the making of this very attractive sign at Denver station which says it all!
23rd August, 1979.

*An impressive sight, here Union Pacific No. 818 **Queen of Wyoming** makes light work moving a fully loaded train around this well landscaped site. 23rd August, 1979.*

Eastbourne Miniature Steam Railway Park.

7¹/₄ inch. Lottbridge Drove, Eastbourne, East Sussex.

The Eastbourne Miniature Steam Railway opened in 1992, the railway following a circular route of about ²/₃rd mile around a large lake. All trains commence their journey from the main station and use scale coaching stock. The Booking Office is near the station and all tickets are clipped prior to joining the train. Adjacent to the station there is a railway-style cafe in a delightful garden setting, a railway wagon souvenir gift shop and toilets. Many facilities include indoor and outdoor model railways, adventure playground, lineside nature walk around the lake, with free picnic areas. Free parking and admission to E.M.S.R. Park.

The ¹/₈ᵗʰ scale locomotive stock comprises 4-6-0 LMS No. 6172 **Royal Green Jackets**, completed by M.Wadey in 1988, a 0-6-0 LMS 4F **No. 4039** by L.J & D. Markwick, 1993 and 2-8-0 GWR **No. 3802**, built by A.Newberry 1988, coming to Eastbourne in 1997. Additionally there is a small 0-4-2T built by M.Wadey, 1982 and a petrol/electric Class 35 Hymek built by M.Wadey in 1986. E.M.S.R. Park is open daily 10am - 5pm from the weekend before Easter until the end of October.

The latest main line locomotive to be added to the stock at Eastbourne is this GWR 2-8-0 No. 3802, photographed here at Shunters Rest whilst on a visit the Rode Woodland Railway on 24th April, 1994.

*With 7¹/₄ inch gauge locomotives, a view at footplate level is most important! This side on view of No. 6172 **Royal Green Jackets** shows considerable detail. 16th July, 1994*

4-6-0 No. 6172 Royal Green Jackets waits deeparture in the station at Eastbourne for the journey around Southbourne Lake. Note the scale goods vehicles, and far left, D7042 Eastbourne Herald. 16th July, 1994.

Echills Wood Railway.   7¹/₄ inch.

Royal Agricultural Society Showground, Stoneleigh Park, Warwickshire.

Echills Wood Railway was constructed in the mid 1970's and is to be found a short distance from the Exhibition Hall. It is a private railway but occasionally runs public services on show days. It was a popular attraction whenever the Model Engineering Exhibition was held there. The return trip is about ¹/₂ mile in length. At the station, Harvesters, a single platform caters for the busy passenger traffic where there is a turntable, sidings and signalling control system. In recent times neat scale GWR signals have been installed on the approach to the station, and colour light signals control the wide road crossing. Beyond, in the wooded area is a second signal box that controls movements over the circuit.

Adjacent to the station a spur provides access to the motive power department During show days a number of visiting engines may add to the excitement of the day!

Leaving the turntable at Echills Wood Railway is a 7¹/₄ inch gauge version of South African Railways 4-4-0 NG 104 Zebedelia. It is based on a SAR locomotive built originally as a 2ft. gauge that operated on a citrus estate at Zebedelia.

Finney Gardens Railway.   7¹/₄ inch.
Bucknall Park, Stoke-on-Trent, Staffordshire.
(Stoke-on-Trent Model Engineers Ltd.)

A new 7¹/₄ inch gauge steam railway was opened officially by the Lord Mayor of Stoke-on-Trent on Saturday, 30th August, 1997. The celebrations attracted a number of visiting locomotives including a blue LMS Pacific No. 46231 **Duchess of Atholl**, nominated to receive the honour of being renamed **City of Stoke-on-Trent** for the day.

The railway is situated in a public park, construction taking place in two phases, the first completed to a very high profile with a covered main line station with two track operation. Nearby are steaming bays and a turntable. Trains leave the station on a long left hand curve to a temporary holding point where a reversal is necessary on to the new river bridge. A further reversal allows through running beyond the station around a long loop in the park, where the train re-enters the station from the opposite direction. The initial length of the railway was ¹/₂ mile; the final phase has now been completed and will provide a 1 mile journey. A second station may be constructed at a later date.

Resident locomotives are Denver & Rio Grande 2-8-0 No. 407 **Old Rube** built by Milner Engineering of Chester.(the second with the same identity), and 0-6-0T No. 6 **Waldenburg**, new from R.Hammond & Son in 1997.

The second phase of the railway was officially opened by the Lord Mayor of Stoke-on-Trent, Councillor Reg. Booth, on 21ˢᵗ August, 1999, the locomotive in service being **Old Rube**.

*The official opening of Finney Gardens Miniature Railway at Stoke-on-Trent was a very busy day with a steam service every few minutes. At the station, No.3 **Ella** was waiting to load up after the departure of resident Denver & Rio Grande 2-8-0 No. 407 **Old Rube**. 30th August, 1997.*

*LMS Pacific No. 46231, here renamed **City of Stoke-on-Trent** for the day's event on the Finney Gardens Railway, was a popular locomotive; no shortage of passengers on the four scale coaches!*

Fort Belan Railway.   7¹/₄ inch.

Dinas Dinlle, Caernarfonshire.

(located west of Foryd Bay via Caernarvon and A499)

Mr. W. Potts opened this short railway during June, 1978 using an 0-6-0 tender engine named **El Meson** based on a 2ft. gauge Bagnall design of 1913. It carried a smart livery similar to Great Eastern blue with red connecting rods; the tender was an eight-wheel version with coal rails, lettered *F.C.COBOS a FURBERO*. The railway was on land outside the enclosed area of the Fort which provided a link with the adjacent car park.

Inside was a maritime museum and slipway, gift shop and cafe. Some of the ancient cannons in the battlement were in working order - these were fired on Wednesday afternoons making a deafening blast of fire power!

By September 1982 a maroon 0-4-2 side tank named **Robert Wynn** worked the line. Both locomotives were built in the Midlands by W.Potts, the former in 1969 and the latter during 1980. The railway operated in a clockwise rotation near the Fort with a run round loop and a turntable at the extremity; the running shed was a timber building near to the entrance gates. The railway had closed by about September, 1983.

*At Fort Belan **El Meson** waits hopefully for passengers during a spell of inactivity. In the far distance are the mountains of Snowdonia. 20th May, 1979.*

*A chilly breeze blows in from the north west. Close to the Fort **Robert Wynn** is about to return sightseers to their cars from this rather exposed coastline. September, 1982.*

Gorse Blossom Miniature Railway & Woodland Park. 7¹/₄ inch.

Liverton, Newton Abbot, Devon.

The attractive Gorse Blossom line is situated in a landscaped setting in a woodland park. The railway is approximately ³/₄ mile in length with one station and open stock.

The railway opened in 1984 using a Lynton & Barnstaple 2-6-2T *Yeo* built by Milner Engineering of Chester in 1979. This locomotive had worked until the previous year at Buckfastleigh on a 7¹/₄ inch gauge railway adjacent to the *Dart Valley Railway* (former name of the *South Devon Railway*).

The railway also operates a Battery Electric Rhaetian Railway Bo-Bo and a petrol locomotive. There are very good refreshments available close to the station. When visiting it is worth noting that Trago Mills 10¹/₄ inch gauge railway is also in the district.

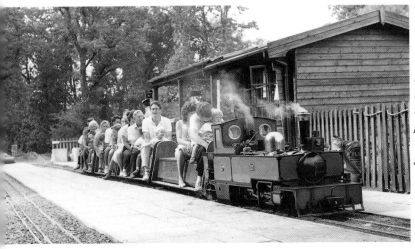

Waiting time at Gorse Blossom. Lynton & Barnstaple 2-6-2T Yeo is ready to leave platform 1 for a journey through the wooded glades. Note the third rail in the foreground. 7th September, 1989.

Great Cockcrow Railway. 7¹/₄ inch.

Hardwick Lane, Lyne, near Chertsey, Surrey.

The Great Cockcrow Railway has been operating for 30 years though its history goes back even further to the *Greywood Central Railway* at Burwood Park, Walton-on-Thames; the home of Sir John Samuel. In the mid-sixties the GCR was moved and the present railway was built on land owned by Ian Allan.

The railway uses all scale locomotives, the operating base is at Hardwick Central and from here there are different routes, all are correctly signalled with semaphore or colour light signalling controlled from three station boxes. The signals are very attractive with good sight lines. The colour lights are self cancelling and some have flashing yellows - unusual if not unique on a miniature railway.

The railway operates on Sunday afternoons, May to October from 2pm until 5.30pm when it is possible to run up to 90 trains, often all steam worked. At Cockcrow Hill a new extension was brought into service at the end of May, 1998. It is a most impressive system with a superb collection of working engines; and it is operated in a very professional manner.

*LMS 4-6-0 No. 6115 **Scots Guardsman** and K5 2-6-0 No. 206 prepare to leave with the 2pm Gladesman from Hardwick Central on 7th June, 1998. Tickets for this train, which traverses the whole railway, can be pre-booked, an unusual facility on a miniature railway!*

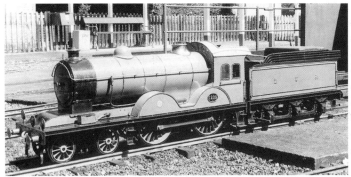

*North Eastern Railway Class R1 4-4-0 **No. 1239** built by Baldwin Brothers dates back to 1913, an attractive engine still lettered G.C.R. on the tender, referring to earlier days at the Greywood Central Railway.*
Hardwick Central, 7th June, 1998.

*LNER K5 2-6-0 **No. 206** stands in the shed yard of the Great Cockcrow Railway awaiting steaming on Sunday, 7th June, 1998. This engine was built in 1956.*

*Royal Scot Class No. 6115 **Scots Guardsman** about to enter Cockcrow Hill station with an afternoon train from Hardwick Central. Here, the locomotive will be turned before returning via Everglades Junction. 7th June, 1998.*

*A rare locomotive to work a passenger train is this War Department 2-10-0 No. 73755 **Longmoor**. In this view the engine is seen approaching Cockcrow Hill station. The route headcode indicates a Down Branch working. Behind the train is Cockcrow Hill signal box; at this point the railway is in sight of the M25 Motorway. 7th June, 1998.*

An early morning shot of LMS 4-6-0 No. 6115 **Scots Guardsman**. *This locomotive had just been pushed outside ready to be steamed for the afternoon trains. The spots on the boiler were from a brief rain shower! 7th June, 1998.*

Grosvenor Park Miniature Railway.

7 ¼ inch.   Chester.

A 7¼ inch gauge miniature railway now graces this beautiful city park, situated only a short walk from the busy shopping area. The railway was opened to the public on 25th May, 1996; the official opening ceremony conducted the previous day when the new line was declared open by Lady Gretton. BBC-North West televised the event.

Initially the railway was intended to operate for one season in conjunction with an exhibition to celebrate the centenary of the Eaton Railway. The superb red liveried 2-6-2 No.10 *Sir Arthur Heywood*, then owned by Brett Rogers, operated services throughout the season. This locomotive was normally based at *Weston Park Railway* but has since been sold to the *Eastleigh Lakeside Miniature Railway* in Hampshire.

The railway forms an oval shape passing over a long bridge alongside an ornamental lake and through tree lined parkland to its starting point. Here there is a trailing spur into the engine shed where the locomotives are serviced. Card tickets are issued from the booking office on the platform.

Outside the exhibition (in 1996) was the 15 inch Eaton Hall brakevan, then on loan from the *Romney, Hythe & Dymchurch Railway*. No.2 **Hilton Queen** ex-*Hilton Valley Railway*, was loaned to the railway in mid-July. The railway reopened at Easter, 1997 using an open cab maroon 0-4-2T **Tinker** built 1994 owned by Malcolm Carroll. A petrol locomotive was also used. The bridge has now been replaced with a more substantial structure and the line has continued as an amenity in this park. The Eaton Hall brakevan has been acquired by the authorities at Eaton Hall where a private 15 inch railway is being considered.

*2-6-2 **Sir Arthur Heywood** was photographed at Grosvenor Park, Chester on 25th May, 1996. The locomotive was in the station where the exhibition was held that year. On the extreme right was the 15 inch gauge Eaton Hall brakevan in restored condition which came from the Romney, Hythe & Dymchurch Railway, and subsequently now at Eaton Hall. **Sir Arthur Heywood** moved in June, 1998 to the Eastleigh Lakeside Railway. When new this engine operated on a railway at Silloth on the Cumbrian Coast.*

Hemsworth Water Park Miniature Railway.

7¹/₄ inch.   Hemsworth, West Yorkshire.

This railway was opened on 24th July, 1993 with an oval circuit of 275 yards. The steam motive power is a 0-4-2T named **Lucy** built by J.Stubbs of Horbury, Wakefield in 1990. Denver & Rio Grande Railroad 2-8-0 No.405 **Utah*** was a visitor to the railway on 7th June, 1994. The railway also operates a Battery locomotive. **Utah** was later sold to the *Swanley New Barn Railway*, renumbered 414 and renamed **Montezuma**, presumably to avoid duplication of identity.

* Another 7¹/₄ inch gauge D&RGR No. 405 named **Utah**, is in private ownership. (see page 136)

*At Hemsworth Water Park Jeff Stubbs Denver & Rio Grande 2-8-0 **Utah** was a visitor to the railway; this locomotive has since been sold and renamed (as there were two with the same identity). 7th June, 1994.*

*The resident locomotive at Hemsworth is Tinkerbell 0-4-2T **Lucy**, built by Jeff Stubbs at Horbury in 1990. This engine had previously operated at Thornes Park Railway, on 8th May, 1994.*

Halton Miniature Railway.   7¹/₄ inch.

Palacefields, Runcorn, Cheshire.

An extensive 7¹/₄ inch gauge railway is situated in Town Park adjacent to the Ski slopes. The line was opened in 1979 and is run by the Halton Miniature Railway Society.   From the station the line follows a route through open parkland with cross loops installed at intervals allowing a reduction in journey length if necessary. At the entrance there are sidings, loading and steaming bays. The railway can be very busy on advertised open days; at other times the service may be worked by steam outline or occasional visiting locomotives. The railway operates in a clockwise rotation. It is quite difficult to locate, follow the signs for the Ski slopes!

*The open days at Halton are sometimes very popular when visiting engines are operating. In this view is 0-4-2T **Louise**, here waiting for the road.*

Hilcote Valley Railway.   7¹/₄ inch.

Eccleshall, Staffordshire. (at Fletchers Country Garden Centre)

Opened in 1993, this popular 750 yard railway is the centre piece of this pleasant garden centre. The railway has a smart landscaped station and booking office; from here trains leave in a clockwise rotation via a loop circuit, providing an enjoyable trip around the lake, then passing through a tunnel before returning to the platform.

The resident locomotives are 1993 built 0-6-0T **Kashmir**, based on a Kerr Stuart Haig class, ex-*Rode Woodland Railway,* arriving at the railway the following year. There is 0-4-2T **Lady Madcap**, and LMS 4-6-0 No. 6141 **The North Staffordshire Regiment**, completed at the end of 1997. A new Tinkerbell 0-4-2 **Primrose**, built by D. Halstead (10/97) entered service in 1998. Special event days operate occasionally with visiting locomotives. Refreshments are available on site. Car Parking.

*A visitor at the Hilcote Valley Railway open day on 14th June, was this BR 0-6-0T No. 1501, also present was BR 2-6-2T No. 84028 and 0-4-0ST **Lady Madcap.***

*Hilcote Valley Railway, Fletchers Garden Centre. An easy place to reach within striking distance of the M6 motorway. This view shows **Kashmir** heading towards the station, 21st August, 1994.*

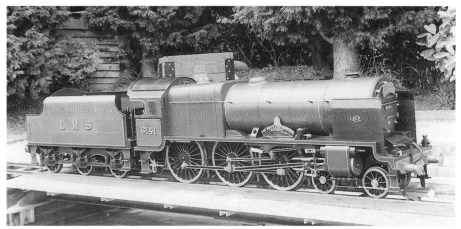

Completed at the end of 1997 by R. Greatrex for use on the Hilcote Valley Railway was this very nice LMS 4-6-0 No. 6141 **The North Staffordshire Regiment***, positioned for the camera on 14th June, 1998. This engine has a North British Locomotive Works plate (Queens Park Works).*

Hilton Valley Railway.   7¹/₄ inch.

Worfield, Shropshire.

The picturesque Hilton Valley Railway with its friendly atmosphere was a photographer's delight, most especially in the early part of the season when the daffodils added sparkle to the wooded glade. It was adjacent to the A454 road from Wolverhampton and became a stop for visitors to the *Severn Valley Railway* at Bridgnorth; a refreshment call where there was always something going on.

In 1957 the Hilton Valley Railway opened to the public; a fare of 9d applied, later increased to 1/-. Hilton station had an overall roof, movements were controlled by colour light signals, and the journey was about ³/₄ mile. The locomotive department was situated close to the station where there was a turntable; used after each trip. The railway followed Hilton Brook to Lawn Pastures and onwards to Stratford Brook which had a grass platform. Here, there was a turning loop; another existed at Lawn Pastures but was seldom used.

On special occasions visiting engines appeared but the railway's own collection of steam locomotives was five in number. No.1 was a Pacific named ***Lorna Doone***, built 1936 by L.Shaw of Ilkeston, No.2 a 2-6-0 ***Hilton Queen***, J.N.Liversage, Herne Bay of 1950. No.3 a 4-8-4 named ***Francis Henry Lloyd***, Guest/Lloyd 1959, and No.7 a 2-6-2 built by S.Battison, 1942. Later came No.9 a 2-8-0 built by Arthur Glaze named ***Michael Charles Lloyd MBE*** of 1975. On a busy Sunday the H.V.R was a hive of activity, trains running signal to signal.

Regretfully, the Hilton Valley is no more. The railway closed at the end of the 1979 season. The infrastructure was moved to Weston Park. There a new line was installed and for a time the Hilton Valley lived again.

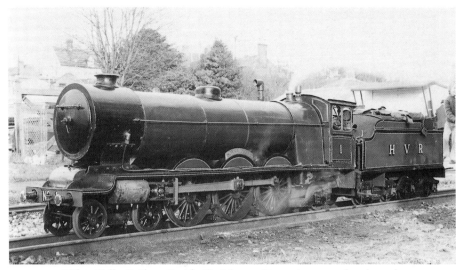

*Hilton Valley Railway Pacific No.1 **Lorna Doone** is prepared and stands waiting for a turn of duty at Hilton station. 6th May, 1979.*

*The Hilton Valley engines always seemed to be well looked after. Here, No.2 **Hilton Queen** waits at a signal check near Stratford Brook on 6th May, 1979.*

*4-8-4 Hilton Valley No.3, **Francis Henry Lloyd** photographed on the return journey on 8th October, 1972.*

*A bright afternoon in early May when the daffodils were at their best. A very popular place to be where parents brought their children for relaxation after the end of a chilly winter. **Hilton Queen** photographed near Lawn Pastures in 1979.*

*The last Hilton Valley steam locomotive built was **Michael Charles Lloyd MBE**. On this occasion, with only a few passengers, the train was returning towards Hilton station. It was a very friendly railway set in really beautiful surroundings. Like all good things it came to an end.   6th May, 1979.*

Little Western Railway.   7¹/₄ inch.

Trenance Gardens, Newquay, Cornwall.

Inland about 2 miles from the town centre of Newquay are the beautiful floral displays of Trenance Gardens. In one corner of the grounds is the 7¹/₄ inch gauge Little Western Railway. The railway forms roughly an oval with a spur near the station to a turntable. In April 1995 Lilliput built 4-6-0 No. 6100 **Royal Scot** was the only steam locomotive. The Scot had a front number plate and nameplates but was unlettered on the tender and cab side sheets. Information at that time indicated some steam working occurred on Saturdays. A Mardyke High Speed Train also operates using two open coaches. The railway is approximately 300 yards in length.

*Little Western Railway Lilliput 4-6-0 No. 6100 **Royal Scot** stands in the sun at Trenance Gardens on 21st August, 1979.*

Manor Park Miniature Railway. 7¼ inch.

Manor Park, Glossop, Derbyshire.

Manor Park is situated about ¼ mile from the centre of Glossop. The railway was originally operated by Mr.& Mrs K. Beeley. The 7¼ inch line opened in 1970 from Manor station forming a circuit through the wooded parkland, crossing a stream twice. The fare was 3d. It had a locomotive shed situated at the end of a lengthy spur from the running line. In 1974 a 2-6-2T *Mountaineer* was obtained, built by Barnes & Thomas at Stalybridge. By 1978 it had been rebuilt as a tender engine doing trial runs on 23rd April. *Mountaineer* moved from Glossop to the *Belton Miniature Railway* at Belton House, north of Grantham. The present location of this locomotive is not known.

In September, 1978 Manor Park Miniature Railway was used to load test Jack Doyle's Class 5 4-6-0 No. 45110; few people knew of this steaming and photographs are comparatively rare of this event. This locomotive had been partially constructed by four people in Manchester and had a Severn Lamb boiler. This Class 5 was sold and is now at the Great Western Railway Museum at Coleford, Glos. The Manor Park Miniature Railway is still active with both steam and petrol locomotives. Normal operation is usually on Sundays.

*One of the resident locomotives at the Manor Park Miniature Railway that simply disappeared was a 2-6-2T named **Mountaineer**. This illustration shows the owner of the engine, Mr.K.Beeley, on 15th May, 1977.*

Opposite: *Scale main line locomotives are not often seen at the Manor Park Railway. On this occasion Jack Doyle's Class 5 4-6-0 **No. 45110** was posed for the official photograph at Manor station in September, 1978. At this time there was only one station; another has been constructed in more recent years at the opposite end of Manor Park.*

Moss Bank Park Railway.   7¹/₄ inch.

Bolton, Lancashire.

A miniature railway operated at weekends at Moss Bank Park, on the north west side of Moss Bank Way, A58 at Bolton. It was opened during August, 1976. The steam motive power was a pair of Hunslet 0-4-0ST's named *Moel Fammau* and *Pendle Witch*, Milner Engineering Nos. 001/002 of 1973/5. The 240 yard line formed a simple circuit through woodland with a spur to the locomotive shed; open stock was used lettered M.B.P.R. The railway had closed by March, 1985.

*Twenty years ago the delights of a little railway could be found in Moss Bank Park, when the sound of a Hunslet could be heard. On this occasion the engine was black liveried **Pendle Witch**, coupled to the driving tender of **Moel Fammau**, 27th March, 1978.*

Myddle Wood Railway.   7¹/₄ inch.

Clover Leasowes, Shropshire.

This North Shropshire 7¹/₄ inch gauge miniature railway opened to the public on specific weekends during the operating season. It had two stations; the main station with an overall roof was adjacent to an attractive scale engine shed. Beyond the station limit was a working GWR signal box complete with a Dutton frame recovered from Llansantffraid (Llanfyllin branch). This controlled full size signals on the MWR main line adjacent to Oak Tree Junction. The railway followed a steeply graded route through open fields, where a second station was under construction on the loop. The engine used the main station turntable after each journey.

Motive power was a black Hunslet 0-4-0ST with driving tender named *Lady Margaret* built in 1986 by D.Munday and coming to Myddle Wood during 1992. Some standard gauge vehicles were also on site, one used as a refreshment bar. The railway has since closed.

*Myddle Wood Railway had a very well constructed main terminal station with a turntable at the end of the centre island platform which allowed access to the engine shed. In the picture is Hunslet 0-4-0ST **Lady Margaret**. 10th April, 1994.*

Ollerton Cross Roads Miniature Railway.

7¹/₄ inch.   Nottinghamshire.

This railway opened about 1952 and was partially hidden in woodland. It formed a circuit of about 200 yards through a clearing and was worked by a LNER A3 Pacific No. 4472 ***Flying Scotsman***, built in 1947 by W.Kirkland. Occasionally BR Pacific No. 60540 ***Earl Manvers***, also from the same builder in 1951, shared the passenger service. The railway operated on Sundays only. A full size signal enhanced the location. It was closed in May, 1977. A previous railway existed on the opposite side of the road from about 1948; operating until the new line opened.

A short distance from Ollerton Cross Roads is Thoresby Hall where Mr. W.Kirkland's 10¹/₄ inch gauge streamlined A4 Pacific No. 4498 ***Sir Nigel Gresley*** operated from 1968 to 1988.

*At Ollerton Cross Roads Miniature Railway. The 7¹/₄ inch gauge No. 4472 **Flying Scotsman** is dwarfed by the full size signal in this woodland setting Although the site was partially screened from the road it was a popular place to visit on Sundays.*

Riverside Miniature Railway.   7¹/₄ in.
Buckfastleigh, Devon.
(Later Buckfastleigh Miniature Railway)

The 7¹/₄ inch Riverside Miniature Railway was situated on a site alongside the standard gauge *South Devon Railway* station at Buckfastleigh. The locomotive was a one third scale Lynton & Barnstaple 2-6-2T *Yeo*, built by Milner Engineering of Chester in 1979. The railway was about ¹/₂ mile in length following a circuit that crossed a substantial bridge in landscaped surroundings. The passenger loading point was adjacent to and convenient for the former GWR station. In 1979 the standard gauge line was known as the *Dart Valley Railway*, and the 7¹/₄ inch gauge miniature railway was the *Riverside Miniature Railway.* The line closed in 1983 and *Yeo* moved to *Gorse Blossom Miniature Railway & Woodland Park.* The Buckfastleigh line reopened during 1993 as the *Buckfastleigh Miniature Railway* with steam and petrol locomotives.

Lynton & Barnstaple 2-6-2T **Yeo** *is seen with a few passengers on the Riverside Miniature Railway. The line was situated close to the Dart Valley Railway station at Buckfastleigh. 19th August, 1979.*

Silloth Miniature Railway.   7¹/₄ inch.

Silloth, Cumbria.   (Solway Firth).

On the grassy banks of the sea shore on the west coast a short miniature railway operated from 1981 until 1988, initial steam working was by a Tinkerbell 0-4-2T named *Valerie* built by K.Williamson, No.3 of 1980, and in 1984 by a new 2-6-2 *Sir Arthur Heywood.*

It was an out and back operation at a fare of 20p return, four open coaches were used. A trailing spur led to the stock shed which had two roads. A petrol and a diesel locomotive worked the line from 1987. *Sir Arthur Heywood* was eventually sold to the *Eastleigh Lakeside Railway,* in recent years it was used at the *Grosvenor Park Railway*, Chester, and on occasions at the *Weston Park Railway.*   At Silloth, the livery was green, similar to *Ravenglass & Eskdale Railway* locomotive *Northern Rock*.

*Almost brand new! A rare view outside the running shed at Silloth of 2-6-2 **Sir Arthur Heywood**, built by K.Williamson & Son, No.3, photographed soon after completion in 1984.*

Photo: Neville Fields

*A breezy westerly off the sea did not deter any passengers, still wearing out of season clothing waiting for **Sir Arthur Heywood**, here, leaving the platform.   In the far distance - sea mist approaching, typical English weather! 26th August, 1984.*

Photo : Neville Fields

Strathaven Miniature Railway.   7¹/₄ inch.
George Allen Park, Strathaven, South Lanarkshire.
(also 5 inch gauge)

The railway is situated within a public park, about ¹/₂ mile from the town centre. The line forms a circuit of about 900 feet which passes through a tunnel following a route around parkland and gardens. The railway was originally built in 1949 by two local men, David Scott and Gavin Hamilton who also built the railway's steam locomotive, a 2-6-0 of *Great Western* appearance, No. 1949, designed by Henry Greenly. The line was operated by Scott and Hamilton until 1956.

The District Council (Forth District) then took over the operation of the railway; still using the same locomotive, which due to failure, was stored in 1964. The Council obtained a 'Warship' diesel outline locomotive designed by David Curwen which continued in use until 1977. The same year the Strathaven Model Society became the railway's operator, repairing the locomotive and track. The track was rebuilt and extended in 1982. In 1999 the railway will celebrate its 50th anniversary. To mark the occasion a further extension is planned to double the length of the line, and already the steam locomotive has been completely rebuilt.

The railway can call upon several other locomotives owned by individual members, brought to the railway as required. These include the superb LMS 4-6-0 No. 6126 **Sans Pareil**; the last engine built by the late Arthur Glaze, and a 4-6-0 Jones Goods along with several narrow gauge locomotives. The railway is dual 5/7¹/₄ inch gauge and has a petrol hydraulic narrow gauge locomotive. Operation is on Saturdays, Sundays and Bank Holiday Mondays from Easter to the end of September.

A similar locomotive to No. 1949 had previously been built for the late Alex Schwab; it is now in private ownership having been rebuilt to a *Southern Railway* outline as **River Itchen.**

On a good day there are quite a number of visitors to the park where 2-6-0 No. 1949 operates. On this occasion the locomotive was kept busy taking families around the nicely landscaped parkland. Quite a dramatic effect was obtained using good quality coal. 31st July, 1994.

Sydney Arms Miniature Railway. 7¹/₄ inch.

Sydney Lane, Crewe, Cheshire.

Sydney Arms Miniature Railway was situated at the rear of the hostelry on Sydney Lane. It opened in 1992 with 125 yards of track and extended in 1993 to its final length of around 285 yards. Trains commenced at an unnamed terminal station, passing Caravan Halt (where passengers could alight to join a 5 inch circuit), then followed the periphery of the field to complete a circle. It was a very pleasant site and all the more remarkable that it was constructed by only four persons. The railway did not operate commercially though a box existed for small donations.

Operation of the railway was normally at weekends and sometimes by steam. One 0-4-0ST oc, was completed by E.Jones named *Laura*, and she became the dedicated motive power and was brought to the railway as required. The railway closed during December, 1995. *Laura* has since visited the *Finney Gardens Miniature Railway*, Stoke-on-Trent at the official opening on 30th August, 1997.

*Sydney Arms, Crewe. Bagnall **Laura** was brought as required to the site. This was quite a nice little friendly railway but its existence was short. 17th April, 1994.*

The Railway Age. 7¹/₄ inch.

Crewe, Cheshire. (Crewe Heritage Centre)

The miniature railway at the Railway Age runs parallel with the West Coast Main Line for most of its length. It has three stations; all trains start their journey at Crewe Old Works station. This station has a roof over the island platform from where the line curves away in a northerly direction, through a short tunnel to Forge End where there is another island platform. The layout is difficult to operate due to a reversal being necessary (after leaving Old Works) at Forge End in both directions; the start of the journey is in effect a branch connection, consequently progress is restricted.

At Forge End station the train engine is removed to run round the stock; occasionally another engine may be waiting to back on to the train. Leaving Forge End, now southbound, it is a straight track to Midge Bridge station. The railway is unusual in having a turntable at each station. The railway opened in June, 1992.

In March, 1994 a 7¼ inch gauge Bassett-Lowke LNWR 4-4-0 No. 1360 **Fire Queen** was put on display inside a glass case. It probably was the one that on occasions worked on the *Hilton Valley Railway.* The locomotive has since been removed.

There are parking facilities prior to entering the site. Refreshments may be obtained at the nearby supermarket.

*Crewe Old Works. A view of a visiting LMS 4F 0-6-0 **No. 43924**; quite an unusual engine on this railway, noted here on 19th July, 1997. The locomotive has since been sold to a private railway in Lincolnshire. Likely to be the only visit of this 4F to Crewe Works!*

*Here 2-4-0ST **Jenny** is ready to return from Midge Bridge station with a fully loaded train amid the clutter of steelwork and overheads of the West Coast Main Line. 25th February, 1995.*

Thornes Park Railway. 7¹/₄ inch.

Thornes Park, Wakefield, West Yorkshire.

Thornes Park Railway is situated in a pleasant woodland location in a large public park, the ¹/₂ mile railway following a double circuit of the parkland. Near the public road is a station, turntable and loading ramp. Initial track laying commenced in 1956. The railway operates from Easter to the end of October every Sunday afternoon from 1400-1730 hours, also Bank Holiday Mondays and occasional Saturdays. Weather and staff availability permitting, winter Sunday trains operate from 1400-1630 hours. In June, 1998 it was the 40th anniversary for continuous operation of a passenger train service. On 3rd May 1999, Bank Holiday Monday, the railway carried a record 1,875 passengers.

Twelve steam locomotives and one American Amtrak diesel are worked on a roster. Usually three engines are in steam in the park and others on display. The locomotive stock comprises two Penrhyn Quarry engines *Linda* and *Charles*, New York Central 4-6-4 No.13 *Hiawatha*, a New York Central 4-8-4 No. 1007, narrow gauge American 2-4-2 No.12 *Alice*, BR Britannia 4-6-2 No. 70008 *Black Prince*, Wren 0-4-0, Greenly 0-6-0T No. 4082, Romulus 0-4-0, Tinkerbell 0-4-2T *Bluebell*, a Tinkerbell 0-4-2T No.14 *Petunia* and an American Virginia 4-4-0, the first 7¹/₄ inch locomotive to run at Wakefield, albeit a visitor to the railway at the time. At the time of writing a new Denver & Rio Grande C19 2-8-0 No. 415 *Li'l Abner* has been built by J.Stubbs at Horbury Works and was available for service during June, 1998. This locomotive was on display at the National Model Engineering Exhibition at Harrogate, 15th April, 1999.

A new Tinkerbell 0-4-2T No. 16 *Victoria* is currently under construction, a Denver & Rio Grande C19 chassis has emerged as No. 417 and to be named *General Palmer*. This is due for completion during 2000/2001. Tinkerbell 0-4-2T *Bluebell* has now been sold to a private owner in Sussex.

Springtime at Thornes Park; a pleasant location and a very friendly railway. Another of the locomotives built in Horbury Works 1994 by Jeff Stubbs, 2-4-2 No.12 Alice. 1996.

*Jeff Stubbs superb LNER B1 4-6-0 No. 1017 **Bushbuck** was photographed at Thornes Park, Wakefield, 1st October, 1978. It was a popular locomotive and now has a new home on a private railway in the Eastern Counties.*

*This 4-6-4 New York Central No. 13 (later named **Hiawatha**) was a joint build by J. Stubbs & I. Hickling. This illustration shows the locomotive soon after completion, working on the inner loop circuit of the Thornes Park Railway on 9ᵗʰ February, 1997.*

Trentham Gardens Miniature Railway

7¹/₄ inch.   Staffordshire

A railway existed at Trentham Gardens during August, 1994 and used a Denver & Rio Grande 2-8-0 No.407 **Old Rube**, built by Milner Engineering, Chester.

The track commenced near a lake and went in a straight line for about 400 yards, trains operating on a pull push arrangement. On a fine Sunday the journey was quite popular with the public. It ran over a few weekends and was later removed, to be reinstated on a permanent site at Finney Gardens, Stoke-on-Trent which opened on 30th August, 1997. There are two identical No.407 **Old Rube** locomotives, the other, the first of the pair to be used commercially, is at the Conwy Valley Museum at Betws-y-Coed.

*Denver & Rio Grande 2-8-0 No. 407 **Old Rube** operating on a miniature line at Trentham Gardens, Staffordshire. 21st August, 1994.*

Walsall Steam Railway. 7¹/₄ inch.

Arboretum Park, Walsall. (off Broadway North via A34 and A4148)

Arboretum Park is a short distance from Walsall. The Railway is 1¹/₄ miles in length with double track formation. It was opened at Easter 1976 by Mr. Colin M.Cartwright as a single line with loops at each end. The initial services were worked by battery locomotives, later joined by a 7¹/₈th inch gauge (later re-gauged to 7¹/₄ inch) 4-6-2 No. 6201 **Princess Elizabeth** built as No. 5065 **Alberta** by Dennis Barton in 1959 and ex - Mablethorpe. The name plate was on the front of the engine. By 1977 two turntables had been installed, one adjacent to the three road shed, the site known as Pathways Halt, the other at Arboretum Central where engines were turned for their return journey.

The late Arthur Glaze loaned his 'GWR' 2-6-2 No.7 to the railway. This engine had an eight wheel tender and had been used on the *Hilton Valley Railway*; and at Lapworth Hall. It was built by Stanley Battison in 1942 and had been rebuilt by Arthur Glaze in 1969. The locomotive stock was gradually increased and LNER A2 Pacific No. 525 **A.H.Peppercorn** was obtained from Arthur Glaze in 1978. A LMS 4-6-2 No. 6230 **Duchess of Buccleuch** was purchased and two *British Railways* 9F 2-10-0's came to the line, No. 92203 **Black Prince** and No. 92220 **Evening Star**. Two LMS Class 5 4-6-0's No. 5000 **Sister Dora** (A.J.Glaze, 1981) and No. 45154 **Lanarkshire Yeomanry** were acquired.

Two other locomotives also appeared at Walsall; the superb GWR 4-6-0 No. 4079 **Pendennis Castle** (built 1976) was an occasional visitor, and LMS 4-6-0 No. 6126 **Sans Pareil**, again both built by Arthur Glaze, the latter in 1986. The Scot was later displayed at the Conwy Valley Railway Museum, protected by a glass case, until sold on 8th October, 1994. By 1997 6201 **Princess Elizabeth** had been overhauled and repainted and she too is now on display at Betws-y-Coed. In 1990 the Walsall Steam Railway was sold to the local council; the purchase included the infrastructure but no rolling stock. The railway has suffered a period of closure but there is a likelihood of operations restarting during 1999.

*LMS Pacific No. 6230 **Duchess of Buccleuch** waits in the old Top Station on the double track section of the Walsall Steam Railway, 28th May, 1978. This section of the railway ran alongside woodland for most of its length.*

*The late Arthur J. Glaze built GWR 4-6-0 No. 4079 **Pendennis Castle** in 1976. Some test running was carried out at Walsall; this view shows the Castle near Arboretum Central.*

*4-6-2 No. 6201 **Princess Elizabeth** is Colin Cartwright's favourite engine. This view shows where the railway emerged from between the trees; at the time devoid of any leaves. April, 1978.*

Weston Park Railway.   7¹/₄ inch.
Weston under Lizard, Staffordshire.
(Weston Park is located on A5)

The railway at Weston Park commenced in 1979 after the closure of the *Hilton Valley Railway*. Most of the track panels had been carefully identified at Hilton Valley so that it would be an easier matter to reinstate them where possible. The present Weston Park line is much longer having two stations with a partial double track layout, the upper section becoming single line with a passing loop, having characteristics of the *Hilton Valley Railway*. The lower end of the railway now crosses a new bridge installed in 1994 and all trains start from the lower station. The railway is now joined with complete turning loops at both ends.

There is a large stock shed adjacent to the railway with a long trailing spur connecting to the running line. On special occasions a number of visiting locomotives may be in use, in recent years the Coleby Simkins Garratt 4-8-2+2-8-4 No. 5928 **Mount Kilimanjaro** (now converted to coal firing) has been used along with 2-4-2 No.25 **Peggy**. Both are privately owned engines. In the past the railway has tended to use a wide variety of motive power whenever possible.

At the time of writing the future of this excellent 1mile long 7¹/₄ inch railway has now been determined. A new operator has been nominated to run the railway; and the frequency of the railway's future operation will be made known in due course.

The EAR Beyer-Garratt No. 5928 was offered for sale early in 1998, along with 2-6-2 No. 10 **Sir Arthur Heywood**. The latter has now been sold to the *Eastleigh Lakeside Railway.*

The sole surviving steam engine from the *Hilton Valley Railway* and still at Weston Park is 2-8-0 No.9 *Michael Charles Lloyd MBE.* There is normally a charge to enter the grounds of Weston Park. Visitor car parking is available by request near to the railway.

*2-6-2 No.10 **Sir Arthur Heywood** was piloted by Fairbourne Railway **Katie** with a mixed set of vehicles including a former Hilton Valley Railway coach. A typical train having traversed the top loop at Weston Park and now returning towards the passing loop and onwards to the station. 2nd September, 1995.*

*East African Railways Garratt 4-8-2 + 2-8-4 No. 5928 **Mount Kilimanjaro** worked at Weston Park after it was converted from oil to conventional coal firing. Towards early evening it was possible to get this massive locomotive out into the sunlight close to the pond for a photo call! Since this photograph was taken it moved north to Scotland for a spell of work on a private railway and has now returned to Weston Park. 25th August, 1997.*

*A rare illustration of the $^1/_3$rd full size 0-4-0 + 0-4-0 Tasmanian Garratt No.1 **Natalia** (named after the Duchess of Westminster) built by John and Stephen Milner, Chester. This immaculate 7$^1/_4$ inch gauge machine was photographed at Weston Park Railway, seen here on 12th May, 1996. This locomotive is currently for sale. The original locomotive was constructed for the North East Dundas Tramway by Beyer Peacock & Co. Manchester, in 1909.*

*It is seldom possible to photograph outdoors the steam miniature locomotives from the National Railway Museum.   At Weston Park, Lynton & Barnstaple Railway 2-6-2T **Taw**, built by Milner Engineering Ltd. was on display on 12th May, 1996, following overhaul work.*

*This 7¼ inch gauge Great Western Pacific No. 8032 **White Fire** was re-gauged from 10¼ inch at the Llanuwchllyn workshops of Bala Lake Railway. As a 10¼ inch engine she was perhaps better known as **Bubbles**. After gauge conversion No. 8032 operated on the now closed Croesor Junction & Pacific Railway at Llanfrothen in a remote part of North Wales. This view shows No. 8032 at Weston Park as a visitor on 8th October, 1989.*

Westby Miniature Railway.   7¹/₄ inch

Maple Farm Nursery, Westby, Lancashire.   (Also 5 inch)

Westby Miniature Railway is located on Moss House Lane, Preston New Road, Westby. The railway is a dual gauge 5 & 7¹/₄ inch system that opened in 1991 in the grounds of the nursery. The station is a substantial wooden structure with overall roof and glass skylights. Adjacent to the station is a turntable and carriage siding. From here the railway is a double line formation for 300ft passing alongside a landscaped pool and waterfall, and connecting to a 630ft circle, allowing trains to operate alternatively in each direction. The length of the track is approximately 1,230 ft. Four sit-aside coaches are used.

A 7¹/₄ inch 4-6-0 LMS **No. 5241** is the usual engine; this was constructed at Ravenglass by Engineer Ian Smith in 1988. There are two 5 inch gauge locomotives, No.3, a Simplex with chain drive and a Hunslet 0-4-0ST No. 20 *Moel Siabod*. Locomotives are removed from the site after use. The railway operates some Sundays in the season. Free travel, donations to offset the running cost.

No. 5241 stands outside Westby Station after working around the circuit on 30ᵗʰ May, 1999.

'Models are an irresistible source of attraction for man. It is the age old instinct to play, an instinct which has quite unconsciously created such great things'

Max Eyth

Worden Park Miniature Railway.   7¹/₄ inch.

Worden Park, Leyland, Lancashire.

This new 5 & 7¹/₄ inch gauge railway was opened by the Mayor of South Ribble on 9th May, 1998. The double track formation connects a public Car Park to the Craft Centre and adjoining cafe area. The operating base where the shed and station are located has steaming bays and a turntable. From here the railway passes over two internal park road crossings, then across open land towards the car parks. Here a very well planned triangle has been installed and there is a dual cross-over on the two running lines. The railway, measured from the turntable to the outer buffer stop is 1207 feet in length. The sleepers have been made from recycled plastic battery containers.

Initial steam test runs were made during early March, 1998. Already interesting locomotives have appeared on test running; including GWR 4-6-0 King No. 6027 **King Charles III,** built by Keith Wilson, and a Hunslet 0-4-0ST No. 4 **Lancashire Witch**; constructed by Halshaw Engineering, of Walton-le-Dale, in 1994.

Two almost identical 0-6-2T's have entered service - quite unusual in this gauge - known as No.1 and No.2. named **Tarique Shelina**, the latter was in steam during the official opening of the line.

Trains operate during the season at weekends and Bank Holidays, other times as required.

*Some test running took place prior to the official opening of the Worden Park Railway. This mid-morning photograph at Leyland shows Great Western 4-6-0 No. 6027 **King Charles III**, amid the superb woodlands of this Lancashire park. The locomotive was built by Keith Wilson. 13th April, 1998.*

Willen Miniature Railway. 7¹/₄ inch.

Lakeside Park, Milton Keynes, Buckinghamshire.

The Willen Miniature Railway was opened in 1988 and has one station, Willen Halt. Here, run round facilities are provided. The operating circuit is about ¹/₂ mile with a spur leading to the locomotive shed. Two locomotives shared the duties, both built by Mr.F.Kenny, 2-6-0 No.1 *Judy* built 1990, and No.2 a 2-6-4T *Ladybird* of 1992. *Judy* has since been sold.

*2-6-4T No.2 **Ladybird** stands in the run round loop. It is quite a large engine with good forward vision. At Willen Halt on 18th September, 1993.*

Opposite Page : *Peter Brotherhood of Chippenham built, in the early 1860s, a 15 inch gauge 2-2-2 locomotive named **Pearl**. This unique engine was loaned for a few days in May 1987 to the Romney Hythe & Dymchurch Railway by the Kings College, London, where it has been on static display since about 1914.*

Courtesy : George A Barlow, BEM.

Index

of locomotive names